GETTING WEALTHY YOUR OWN WAY

AMUSA ABDULATEEF

AUTHOR OF **JOBS WITH ZERO CAPITAL VOL. ONE & TWO**

(C) AMUSA ABDULATEEF (2016)

Visit www.amusa-abdulateef.com for our other books on different issues.

+234 80 5671 0944   **+234 80 3215 5018**

addinrv@gmail.com   latlib222@yahoo.com

© **No part of this book should be reproduced in any form or version, stored in a retrieval system or transmitted by any means, manual or electronic, for any purpose, without the written permission of the author.**

AUTHOR'S MIND

The reputable and bestselling author, **Brian Tracy** books especially '**Getting rich your own way**' motivated me into writing beautifully. **Dale Carneggie** '**How to make more friends and influence people**' remains my mentor. The books changed my thinking. Research shows that the nations and the nationals of poor nations, like those in the developed nations, also have the huge potentials to become wealthy in the nation without travelling out of the shores searching for green pastures. The only pointer to making the wealth is the opportunities that are always available at the beck and call of the thinkers. Many do not know that people that face challenges at a time used to be successful in their life endeavours especially of interests. Those who are successful usually face the hardest of times. In such nations where they lived at the time, there were challenges that could send people into untimely grave but yet they make breakthrough. The gathered information from the biographies and interviews thought me how to meditate deeply into problem-solving research which helps to identify ways people can get wealthy their own ways..

In view of the above, I research on how people can get rich their own way using the language of the revered author, **Brian Tracy**. By getting wealthy in one's way, we do not only mean 'being rich in money', we equally mean 'ability to enrich one's knowledge and skill first and then the earning to move up from low income earner to big earner which keeps growing by the day. The knowledge is the basic need to boost income from the noble saying of the noblest 'he who desires this life (its alluring materials), seek knowledge, he who desires next life should seek knowledge and he who desires both should seek knowledge'. On the flip side, people by their attitudes to learning new things, irrelevant values being adhered to, poor decisions and unjust allocations of resources make themselves poor. Simply say, there are ways, by common sense measures, that people, institutions and governments are and can render themselves poor. It is by their own self-inflict. A nation whose recurrent expenditures keep rising over the capital budget at the time the social infrastructures to build wealth are dilapidated or grossly inadequate has invited indigence to the nation. A nation that prefer to invest in a sector at the peril of others is running at the brinks of becoming poor. How can a nation be solely depending on the earning from a sector? What would happen if the sole export becomes valueless in the local and international markets? How do we classify a man that values his ethno-religion 'values' or personal ignorant-based interest to be wealthy in the present world? A man whose wife is a fulltime housewife faces the risk of losing the children and the wife to the streets at the time his only source of income dropped or when his limbs are too feeble to work again due to unforeseen circumstances like sudden ailments, accidents or even old age.

Without mincemeat of words, lack of vision, poor planning on the available resources instead of planning what someone (individual, institution, association, club, philanthropist, nation) promised, lack of financial discipline, poor vision and misallocation of funds and other resources are gateway to being poor. We can summarize the epistle thus -a major cause of poverty of people, institution and government is lack of knowledge that brews poor attitudes to issues on what to spend, how to spend and the path to undertake to achieve what is to gain from investments of time, money and other resources in order to grow the wealth. Nations lose billions to other nations through the huge consumption of foreign goods and services. Such freely thrown open the markets for all sorts of goods and services. Outsourcing has crippled the intellectual capacity of the local people not knowing that they would suddenly become poorer when the nations supporting them in all the needs decide not to sell again by cutting the economic ties. From our studies, nation should build upon her areas of strength. For instance, nation should be solve the problems of the basic needs for its people. The people must be able to eat balanced diets, live in decent houses and wear clothes of choices that suit different occasion at affordable cost. Additional basic needs are the quality education, health care services, communication and transportation. When these are easy and affordable if not gratis to the people and institutions in a nation, then the people have the opportunities staring their faces to grow their wealth at their choice pace, space and time. The profit-and non-profit based businesses owned by both the public and private proprietors, that are inevitable to the aggregate growth of an economy of a nation, should enjoy flexible and periodically reviewed policies that would suit the demands of the dynamism in the markets within and globally. This process shall enhance their business growth aside the cheap aesthetics in the business environment provided by the government as their own basic needs. With these in place, wealth is creatable and would constantly soar in growth by the overall contributions of motivated individuals, quality and more focused institutions and visionary leaders at all positions of authorities at all the tiers of governments. Expectedly, the national aggregate in growth would forever remain positive that would advance the nation into one of the fastest growing in wealth creation. Failure to be up and doing, the reverse is the case Read under 'spices'. The latter are ignorance of how to use the resources at their disposal. The compilations of works shall expose readers into such ways to become millionaire or poorer within a short space of time of few months.

Let the readers read with full attention and be free from the scourge of unemployment and earning the same income. The value added jobs in the book are the limitless creatable value chains of the sectors of the economy that would add to the income of individuals and institutions. Keep reading. Keep learning. Make your choices, add new jobs, increase your sources of earning income and grow your incomes to become a millionaire. This is a mission that is highly feasible. Nations and institutions could generate more incomes from the forward and backward integrations. What do we mean by this? They could start earning more from looking back and thinking for future. The present challenges and what the future should look like are the platforms for the generation of more revenues for the nations and profits for the business institutions. **Getting wealthy your own way** is an irresistible and an eye-opener material with first-hand experience stories. Unemployed graduates have no reason for not having business ideas to start earning and growing their wealth of knowledge, skill and money. The contents are not just for individuals, but for institutions and nations to develop from the poor to rich by their choices. The third chapter is the main thing. It established the fact that individuals, institutions and governments choose to be either wealthy or poor. There is no one to blame for being poor but self by the revelations in the book. The contents of the work are majorly based on biographies, interviews and different experiences and studied profiles of different people, institutions and governments. Study the paragraphs carefully and invent several good business idea- Author (2017)

DEDICATION

Dedication to my humble family members especially my lively kids Abdulaziz Ayomide and Sheriff Ayokunmi

ACKNOWLEDGEMENT

Appreciation goes to the Creator who endows the writer with knowledge of researching into proffering solutions to issues of global importance. My next whole hearted gratefulness goes to the courageous family that provides the right atmosphere for my intellectual property to develop and become materials that impact lives. Special thanks to the fans globally. I salute the supports of my spouse, Kudirah Joy Oladipupo and her children, Abdulaziz Ayomide and Sheriff Ayokunmi. My appreciation to the likes of Mrs Anike Abe and her hubby, Pastor Abe and their children is eternal just as Mrs. Tomilayo Laniyas, Mrs. Felicia Modupe Adeleke, Mr. Bayo Olafusi of this world.

The supports from the friends like Surveyor Abdulramon Abubakar, Bro. Abdulkabir Oladiti, Mr. Tunde Yusuf of Techmanit Technology, Mr. Babatunde Olajide Yusuf of Omic Technology, Mr. Olalekan Joel Awujoola of Nigerian Defence Academy Kaduna, Mr. Biodun Jimoh Tiamiyu of Nigeria International School, Cotonou, Benin Republic, Mr. jimoh Oseni Folayemi of Odigbo Local Government, Ondo state among others.

I salute the courageous and material supports of my in-laws within and abroad in the persons of Alhaji Bashir Oladipupo Adebisi and his spouse, Mrs. V.O.A Adebisi, Mr. Babatunde Oladipupo among others..

THE PREAMBLES

In the books we wrote on entrepreneurship, we pointed out the fact the ignorance of people about information around has been a major cause of unemployment. There are opportunities for people living in the underdeveloped and poor nations to tap from to become self-employed with ease. The advanced nations have apparently reached their peaks in the employment generation unless they have special packages for new investors with new ideas for creation of new jobs from the existing jobs and structures. In all the worlds, developed, developing and the underdeveloped nations, the level of thoughts and intellectual brilliance would play major roles in the amassing more wealth as one desires. In the advanced nations where there is limit of hours to work, some still outsmart the structure by working for more hours. Some migrants in the nations used to claim to work in the factory as guards at night after working as cab operators in the day. The two jobs could on hourly basis. It is easy to have a lawyer who runs reality shows on television station, serving as consultants to executive officers of company, be an active human right activist or their legal officer and even acting in films or major promoter for entertainment firms. In the other nations of developing and the underdeveloped, in most cases, the businesses that are combined with others are the retailing and the earnings could not be as big to meet the basic needs. One thing in the mind of all that are involved in different jobs is to amass more than enough for the basic needs in order to have savings for further investments. This is the reason for learning how to imbibe the habit of saving, bootstrapping and have interest in investing so much in information and communication technology as the products and services are the most sought for in the world. The poor nations are spending trillions of dollars to have all the products and services from the knowledge-based courses. On the other hand, all citizens and non-indigenes residing in the developed nations have access to wi-fi environment and cheap infrastructures especially access to information and communication at a very cheap cost. Through them, the level of thinking is very high unlike in the poor nations. In the climes, employments are easily generated for the people abroad from the value chains. The value system of most of the poor nations could deprive them of getting wealth their own ways but the reverse could be the case. In Nigeria value system especially of the burying culture and marriage, the southern tribes used to spend huge sum of money that could eat deep into their capital. Some do not mind borrowing to fund funeral ceremonies or to fulfil a religion obligation which is not the tenet of the religion. In the nations, one man's food is another man's poison or may we say that different windows open to the world. When certain parts of the globe is in darkness, the other parts are in broad daylight. Studies from the imbalance of trade, the running of budget deficits where fiscal budgets are run through borrowing from creditors or selling of assets, the borrowing or debtor nation suffers the heat. It would not be an easy task to make wealth at one's pace unlike in those creditor nations. In short, the approaches or the ways of getting funds and manpower for the smooth running of the new businesses in the poor nations used to create wealth for investors of the existing ones abroad as these are in the 'deliberate' crippling economy, unstable political systems in the poor nation by introduction of strange policies. The poor and apparently hopeless business environment is forcing the locally produced potentially 'quality' manpower to flee the poor nations for green pasture abroad. The poor nations that lack visionary leaders would continue to groan in poverty if the leaders fail to understand how to create and grow the wealth. Such nation in economic crises is bereft of true visionary leaders who lack intellectual capital to lead the nation aright. They fail in the churning out of policies just like private business institutions. By so doing, there is brain drain in the poor nations and brains gains for the wealthy nations. Quality manpower would move away to better companies who can pay for their technical ability and quality in service delivery. The corrupt leaders in the poor nations have safe tax haven in the nations abroad. Once the loot is diverted to the foreign accounts, the beneficiary nations could use the fund to support the economies and their investors, researchers and others have enough capital for investment. The nations where the money has been looted have substandard education, medical, transportation, security services while the beneficiary nations abroad have the service in quality and abundance. What an irony of life! The books we referenced to show how one can boost one's idea with the use of other people's money, materials, methods, machinery and market among others to make positive business impacts on the owners and the nation in general. It is easy to enhance one's wealth with the conversion of an office into offices, a business to accommodate more businesses, a spacious and adequately equipped station hosting many stations, stores in stores and services in a service station. By so doing, one would get wealthy in one's way and at one's pace. This has been the purpose of writing this book.

From our studies and clear indicators from the effective use of information available at our fingertips, all sectors of the economy across all the shores of the world have their endless value chains to turn the nations either wealthier or poorer depending on the policy statements and implementation. And if a company is wealthy, the think tanks leading the pack are wealthy of knowledge and managerial skills including discipline, principles of organization or management to pursue the right tracks to meet their vision and mission statement of the business. In such company, there is great tendency that the employees are also well remunerated to have enough savings as disposable for investments on personal ideas. The market situations also have their own values on the making either the wealthy or otherwise of the individuals, institutions and the state in general. Each market situation that is most common or popular in a nation or business environment influences how to get rich by one's degree of inputs and the levels of sustaining the soaring of the wealth. In the poor nations leading by corrupt and selfish leaders, the bigger the vacuum or the bridge between the rich and the poor, the more the wealth of the rich and the poorer the poor. At those nations, there is inequality in the society. The business of the rich are highly patronized by the government and people whereas the poor enjoy no or very slow patronage. The rich could enjoy tax waiver unlike the poor. The businesses of the rich are insured unlike those of the poor. The differences are limitless depending on the people at the helms. In the nations of the world, the wealthy ones used to donate big to the campaign of the leaders and suffice the reason for the supports they got from the government when they assumed the positions of authority.

In all facets of business decisions, incomes can be earned legally from newly introduced complementary jobs. This is possible from the arts of production and improving services for service-based jobs. Just like creating new jobs from the existing jobs, new chains of values can be created from the existing value chains from identifiable sectors. The economic sectors usually have the production or service and marketing sections. The former are producers and the latter are the sellers. The sellers could be those within or said to be under contract or could be from the independent chain of the marketing. From the studies, sellers are in multiples of the makers. A company may have 100 employees and the products from the company is sold by indirect employees running to several thousand across the globe. A farmer could provide indirect jobs for 1000 persons in promoters, transporters, distributors, bulk sellers and retailers from his produce of food, cash crops and raw materials to feed industries within and outside. This is not added to those people or businesses that convert the materials or produce from farms into another finished goods outside the agro-allied businesses like the manufacturers, processing companies, packaging firms, brand makers, media stations for publicity among others.

By the title, we mean getting rich at your own pace and timeline with the use of the information at hand. The samples are countless. Many coal sellers could partner with a coal pot builder at an agreed selling price and discounts on sales for the coal seller who owned the shop. This enables her to have the two complementary products at the same shop. The stock would remove the stress of the coal buyers to distance apart where the coal pots could be got. In some cases, some customers would decide to be using the coal at the absence or scarcity of fuels and gas when the complementary products are at the same shop. As she is making money from the coal, she would making extra gains from the selling of the coal pot. This is creating one-stop shop. Through the one-stop shop or multi-departments stores in a store or station, customers would trickle to the shop to make purchases. One can imagine the profits from different departments of the owner. But in some cases, the owner of the big store may not be able to have all the complementary products. The proprietor should engage in supplies partnership with the makers or the accredited distributors from the brands makers.

In all the climes, it is easy as a, b, c to increase one's wealth and vice versa. The prevalent challenges facing a nation could be the sources of increasing the revenues for such nation. Let us cite some instances. A nation that is backward in the use of knowledge-based economy could decide to explore the opportunities on ground to turn its economy on the path of growth through the sector. Those who are monolithic economy could start the diversifications into other sectors to earn more. Cuba in some years past developed their medical sector to the extent that the nation had exports of medical professionals outside the nation. It also invested so much in boxing that Cuban coaches became toast of the world. Brazil is known, just like all the South America nations, is known with football talent exports to the top leagues in Europe. The availability of talented and skillful football players across the world is an indicator that football business through a better packaged football league across divisions could fetch any nation forex and several thousand if not millions of employment aside boosting all other sectors like aviation, financial, insurance, fashion, processing or confectionery, road transportation, hospitality, medical institutions, tax authority, arts, photography, media-based jobs, entertainment, textile, publishing, printing among others. European nations especially United Kingdom has turned football management into a major sector that has boosted several sectors as listed. The newly packaged English Premiership League since 1992 is richer than many nations. The stakeholders in the leagues are earning in millionaires on weekly basis not to talk of all sectors that are added values to the competitions. Each of the owners of the twenty teams in the league are multi billionaires. Many of them are foreign investors and the players are from all over the world. One can imagine what the other forms of sports that are rebranded like football league could be fetching the nations across the globe. And the management of the league would not stop in making more attractions that would turn the sport into the biggest earners for the nations, investors and the other stakeholders like the players, the coaches or the technical crews, the financial sectors, the medical institutions among others. All nations need to search for useful information about any sector to turn the table in favour of themselves to earn more. If a nation is earning 2 billion dollar annually in a sport, one can imagine how much it could be making if it rebrands at least five other sports like athletics, lawn tennis, table tennis, golf, horserace or polo, swimming, boxing or any other forms of the indoor sports. It would be attracting investors from within and the flexibility in the packaging would attract investors from outside the shores. What would those foreign investors bring to the economy of the host? Of course, huge sums of money and their technical input. Through rebranding of the English Premiership League today, investors on each of the club in the league are from all races and continents of the world. The French league popularly called 'ligue 1' is also attracting investors from abroad. The purchase of star players who are talents and skillful in the round leather game including the seasoned coaches who are always thirst for silverware, the procurement of firm referees and the beautiful stadium aesthetics are some of the ways to brand a league. The media hype should not be under emphasized.

With these in place, the sport has become a platform to increase the earnings of the nation from direct earnings and the attraction of more investments that are added values from the value chains of organizing football contests. In England, all the cups are sponsored by big and multinational companies in order to promote their products and services to the huge fans and others in the nations. Stadiums of the teams in the league are sponsored and manage by investors. The insignias of the teams are investments that are generated income for the owners, the players and the institutions not to talk of the various forms of taxes that are coming to the coffers of the state or the nation. If a player is asked to endorse a product, or selected to advertise a service or product as a face of the product or service, such would be earning for himself, the club he belongs and the nation where the club is located. In short, opportunities to get wealthy at one's pace is at the fingertip of individuals and institutions. Each time any friend who has a running business is complaining about low sale, I used to tell them to think within and outside the box. No business can exhaust the ever-existing potentials available from the prevalent conditions that would not increase the source of income. In fact, this has been the subject of this book from outset. Opportunities to be earning in multiples of the present earnings is with the think tank in each sector for the nation and institutions. The degree of the use of available information matters. Studies show that most business owners that have decline profits or no profits or in the part of a nation, the depleting external reserves and soaring debts are those with one source of income. We call this in economic parlance as the nation running monolithic economy. Any nation that has diversifications would earn income from all the sectors. In case there is drop in the earning of some products in the markets, the incomes from others would stabilize the economy and the impact of the decline would not be felt by the nation and its citizens. The same is applicable to business institutions. In a conglomerate business, some products, particularly the fast moving goods, used to be the cash-cows that would be supporting the others. The other products would enjoy internal economies of scale to There would always be the 'most liked products' among the lines of products from the same company. It is possible for the business to set its priority right targeting getting more wealth through right diversification otherwise there could be problem to the going-concern of the business. As this is with the business, individuals can grow or reduce the amount of their wealth if they fail to apply the information as it should be applied.

Several lessons are learnable from the contents of the work. There must be brave steps that must be taken. Set timeline for your arrival as one of the wealthy persons in your community. The timeline set is a function of personal financial and moral discipline in social life. Somebody who does have financial discipline may never have limits in spending. They used to overspend beyond budgets even if they have one. This is done by the improving on the creativity level of the person. Out of all challenges are opportunities for the creative minds to make a breakthrough. Let me cite the issue of economic recession in nations. The moral lessons from the recession are the increasing of the sources of income of people, the cut of the expenses on luxurious goods and services, the saving for a rainy day, moving along the dynamics of the business environment especially the economic policies of the government. In such periods in the history of nations, opportunities are there for institutions and individuals including the governments to boost employment-revenue generations.

If all the lessons are worked upon in the minds of the individuals and businesses, then there would not be a time of severe decline in the economic activities. If the new economic policy of the government is import substitution; and the right inputs are provided in order to make the business operating environment become enabling, then he who dreams of getting wealthy in his own way must quickly key to the projects and grab the selected opportunities that would bring the highest returns. On the other side, readers would see how people become poor as they choose by their ignorance.

TABLE OF CONTENTS

TITLE PAGE

AUTHOR'S MIND

DEDICATION

ACKNOWLEDGEMENT

PREAMBLES

CHAPTER ONE

SPICES

ECONOMIC SECTORS AND THE VALUE CHAINS

CHAPTER TWO

OPPORTUNITIES FROM THE VALUE CHAINS

CHAPTER THREE

GETTING WEALTHY YOUR OWN WAY

GETTING POOR YOUR OWN WAY

CHAPTER FOUR

GAINS TO THE NATIONAL ECONOMY

CHAPTER FIVE

BOOSTING THE SECTORS IN THE TIME OF RECESSION

CHAPTER SIX

EMPLOYMENT GENERATION AND IMPROVING STANDARD OF LIVING

ABOUT THE BOOK

ABOUT THE AUTHOR

CHAPTER ONE

SPICES

Visit the open markets and the malls. In the former, products from the farms and local factories are in the largest percentage. In the latter, there are more foreign goods with only a few locally made goods. The consumers, even the poor, prefer the foreign goods known as 'tokunbo' or by literally meaning 'the fairly used' from abroad. Visit schools and closely observe the people at public places like markets; take a stock of the accessories being wore by individuals, the vehicles being run on the roads, the domestic needs at homes and offices…; it is obvious that the foreign items are not less than 70%. Buying imported goods by consumers does not promote the growth of national wealth. These consumers are individuals, institutions and even the government ministries, departments and agencies. They prefer to buy these items than paying for the fairly used of the locally made goods. And there is no legislation against importing fairly used goods. By purchasing both the new and the fairly used from abroad, where and how would the local firms be able to grow their wealth? If the schools are importing books and instructional materials from abroad, how would the local firms grow their income? Such amount of money for importation of the new and the fairly used goods are injections to the nations abroad and a huge withdrawal from the local economy. By this, the volume of currency, the legal tender, in circulation in the nation would be very small compare to what is withdrawn from the circulation through the huge purchases from the malls. Let us use simple Mathematics for illustration. If the total consumption in money within is 5 billion and the total amount of the foreign goods imported as new or fairly used amounts to 3 billion. It shows that only around 2 billion would circulate the economy or serves as the amount with the people while around 3 billion has gone to serve foreign economies. I made it clear to my spouse that the bulk of the money that are supposed to be circulating the economy are going out through sports betting and all forms of gambling, the huge consumption of foreign goods, the patronage of foreign services both at the peril of the local goods and service, outsourcing of expatriates from abroad at the expense of the employment of the local manpower, paying employees and estacodes on foreign currencies, the weak anti-money laundering policy, poor debts servicing of the nation that attracted stringent borrowing conditions by the negotiators of the government among others. I told her about the attitude of those who looted the nation and keeping the huge sum in their wardrobes, abandoned houses and farms simply to avoid being captured by the Bank Verification Number (BVN). All the looted funds kept in different places are supposed to be parts of the currency to be in circulation if such money truly served the purpose of their withdrawn from the federation account. Instead of executing the designated projects that money were appropriate for, the corrupt elements diverted the sum into their illicit personal accounts in their homes. She itched to know more when she complaint about her friend who was in debts that had almost become hypertensive. I responded 'Your friend is the enemy of her progress. She became indebted as a result of her ignorance about cost of capital she got from micro finance banks to run her business and her extravagance lifestyle. Here was a trader that was repaying the loans with high interests on weekly and monthly basis not to talk of her over budgeting. She was not modest in spending and lacked good plan. How can a business income of about 5,000 naira be sustaining three square meals aside the other basic needs of almost ten persons on a daily basis? Each of the dependents cannot spend less than 500 naira for the meals alone not to talk of the other essential expenses on a daily basis. Already the business is bound to run bankrupt from outset. In medical parlance, it is a business 'dead on arrival' (DOA) or 'brought in dead' (BID). Would such business survive? Can we say that such a weekly repayment a good loan to run a business? How would a business whose profits are growing by 5% be paying for capital with interest of 25%? She was a victim of exploitation of the micro finance bank. Such loans had been non-performing loans (NPLs) from outset! Her business had died on arrival with the use of such high interest capital. Secondly, findings showed that she invested the capital sought for the business in property that would not fetch her any profit but a liability. It is expected that property should be executed from the part of the gains from the business and not with the capital that was supposed to be invested to earn profits. What can we draw from the two scenarios narrated? In an economy that is in distress, the number of beggars increase. <u>They choose to be beggars</u> because they are bereft of lofty idea on how to start small businesses and grow their little income at outset. I was told of a jobless fulltime housewife and mother of four kids that lost her breadwinner husband suddenly. Unfortunately, the husband left no pin to inherit. She was like a nation that suffers loss of revenue in a sector that used to be the cash-cow who therefore resorts into begging from rich nations for sustenance. For how long would such be begging for means of sustaining the family and the citizens respectively? Would that be forever? There must be series of solutions to select from. And the solution is in grabbing choice opportunities around to be free from begging to survive. The widow could start hawking business of groundnut, fruits, maize and several other consumable foods. These are businesses she could start with as low as 1,000 naira. In many cases, she could get the product on sales on return from those who are into the business. There are caterers beside the motor parks that need hawkers. There are food canteen owners that require shop attendants. There are those in hospitality business that need waiters, launderers and messengers. There are homes and offices that need cleaners and maids. Many sole proprietors always seek the services of unskilled people, male and female. With dedication to work and a strict financial discipline where art of saving has become a habit of such persons. A nation that has dwindling income from its cash-cow needs to diversify while it releases policies that would boost the sectors of the economy. All products are potential cash-cows depending on the level of wealth and the rate of growth. If the nation, just like individuals and institutions must cut their expenditures at the time of declining revenues, new policies that would trigger all the sectors to be generating more revenues should be created. Repackaged sports sector, for instance, could boost the income generation of the nation not excluding the employments for the unemployed in the nation through the improved Gross domestic product and hence the Gross national Income. We have used this example in the repackaging of English Premiership League since 1992. The football sector, just as in United Kingdom, in Spain is a major backbone to the wealthiness of the nation according to an executive officer from Spanish La Liga during a visit to Nigeria recently. All nations could collaborate with brands to increase the national wealth. Let us look at the tourism sector, through the collaboration of the tourism board with sports department, nations would boost the number of tourists and the income from all sectors like publishing and printing of souvenirs, hospitality, transportation, communication among others to the nations. In the world of today, sports play huge sum of money to bid for the hosting of sporting events. One can imagine the amount of forex being paid by the nations to host world football contests. Did the nations that pay such huge sum to host do that without target benefits? The simple target is the sure way of improving the economy and turn the nation to the position of advancing nations. To achieve this, right policies must be in place. With right policies, steps and strategies by the nations, individuals and institutions respectively supported by zero-tolerance to corruption in any form in the quality and unbiased implementation to the letter, the wealth shall start growing. Lack of knowledge and the obvious reasons to grow income is a matter of choice. Individuals, institutions and governments could decide to grow their wealth of knowledge and riches if they decide and vice versa. If a trader is able to study market, his business proposal should indicate the types of loans with interests that could be obtained. The government representatives must work out the feasibility and performing loans if obtained. A business that runs its activities with non-performing loans particularly those loans with very high interests and unfavourable conditions must avoid them. The conditions on ground is not a yardstick to resign to fate. Disability does not mean inability to start earning and growing wealth of knowledge, skills and riches. 'A lack' does not mean 'nothing' by our operational definition. It only means 'temporarily not available'. It is an eye opener to create. Lack of wealth does not mean wealth is not available in disguise or cannot be created provided they do not back the wrong horse. It is insufficient idea and failure to apply inputs or use the opportunities to start generating wealth. Wealth can be continually created and can be done after all it has been proved beyond doubt that many capital-intensive jobs could be started with zero-capital! (See details in **Jobs with zero capital Vol. One and Two** by the same author)

ECONOMIC SECTORS AND THE VALUE CHAINS

Churned out policies from the people at the helms determine whether a nation would grow its wealth or otherwise. The also applies to all institutions. I could recall several challenges thrown at us during my tertiary school days brought about the attitudes into research in me today. I could still vividly recall that a poser from a lecturer brought about writing the book "Creating new jobs from the existing jobs". Many students in the tertiary institutions have been earning money from the use of their intellects in the identification of money making opportunities. Visit to the hostels and you would find the student barbing salon, the dry cleaning service, the shoe cobblers, the stylists, the sellers or hawkers of boutique, cosmetics, jewelries, among others by the students regardless of the gender and age. Some are into typesetting job to earn money. There are those who ride commercial rides to earn stipends. Before they leave the schools, they have built right brands. In the book "wastes to wealth jobs", it sounds ridiculous to the writer of nations with very large challenges that are sources of making wealth and still seeking for donor nations to run the government. Each poor nation in Africa chooses to be poor as most of them are naturally endowed with both human and non-human resources. Mention a nation and I would tell you numerous opportunities to be wealthy and never be poor. One fact that is common to most poor nations is that their leaders at one point poor the other are richer than their nations. Individuals who had been in positions of authority had looted the nation for selfish reasons. Among the billionaires of the world are the leaders from the nations. With the eradication of selfish amass of wealth for personal use, the economies of the nations would sustain unborn generation. What did they use the arable lands for? What are the benefits of the intellectuals being churned out of different institutions in the lands? All sectors in the national economy have numerous value chains depending on the nature of flexibility and dynamism of the business environment. An environment that has high consumption rate presents huge opportunities for individual, proprietors, management to boost their wealth vice versa. There is the need to get adequate information about the business environment before the open opportunities are identified and explored at one's pace. The chains are up to create limitless employment opportunities towards spreading the wealth of the nation. Studies show that value chains of agriculture include the provision of raw materials for industries to proliferate. One can create new materials from those existing value chains from farms. What do I mean? Let us look at the textile industries. A designer could design different styles of wears from the use of clothing materials got from the market. Such could demand for customized materials as fabric to design variants of materials for their special very important personality customers. From farms are harvested cotton for textile factories; rubber for plastic factories and tyre industry; pulp is from the forest for paper mills; the food crops for processing industries, the cash crops for the beverages and related companies, the medicinal herbs, saps and barks for pharmaceutical firms, shea-butter and the likes for cosmetic firms, and the planks for construction companies, wood-based decors, carpentry and furniture accessories. If we critically look into the other sector in the extractive and exploring industry like mining, several factories evolved creating employment opportunities and wealth distribution.

A nation with prevalent challenges have thrown open avenues to creating more wealth. In the book from our stable 'Artisans and artisanship', we revealed how they are lowly paid from poor negotiation has been the bane of earning little capital for the reinvestment in value added jobs. Many local artisans fail to add new jobs such as supplies of the materials needed to boost the revenues. Let us cite more samples. An electronic repairer should be selling the parts. The vulcanizers should have tubes, tyres, grease and other parts. Each of these are separate income earning. All accessories being sold and serviced by technical-based services are openers to earn revenues and therefore move up the scale. What about the institutions? Someone who is into catering of snacks has the opportunities to be baking loaves of bread and related to open the chances of earning more.

Many a 'mushroom' school has the potential to grow their income through hard work and dedication to duties of the staff. Mushrooming of schools is the same as proliferation of schools and not about the quality of the staff, especially the teaching staff that would impact the knowledge and the skills to the pupils. A good business is always imitated by other people but the uniqueness in the management and day to day running of the business would distinguish the level of earning income. A school could improve its income from the introduction of after and pre-school services. Some could introduce extra-curriculum activities to make more income. A retailer may engage in home delivery after notification of the target buyers in its list of customers. It is odd and old ways of retailing business to stay static in a place of sale. Instinct should guide the retailers to join home delivery or supplies rather than waiting for buyers from the passers-by. In a community where social interaction and values are revered, it is easy to increase the number of enrolment hence the possibility of making more income from parents and institutions who have wards in the school. I submitted several means by which a school running into debts could making huge revenue from the tail of the year end of the year party. In the school, there are several businesses that would add values to the service which would surely add to the income. Some of these are under 'catch them young series' for all categories of pupils in different ways.

Just as government can diversify to improve the revenue base of the nation, the institutions could be made strong and independent to earn bigger. What about individuals who are proprietors and proprietresses of businesses? Government could open new sectors from the existing sectors, create new institutions from the existing institutions for the diversification and sources of adding to revenue generation. In the book "Economic recession, the causes, the trends, the spiral adverse effects and the practicable solutions' from the same author, we highlighted different means of generating billions to the coffers of the government. The reforms advised to be introduced to make the institutions stronger are avenues to boost the wealth of the nation. For instance, if the book and intellectual property agency under the ministry of education is independent, it could be an avenue to shore up the income of the nation. The technical departments of the security agencies, if adequately equipped, could build arms and ammunition for the nation and export. Instead of budgeting huge forex to import ammunitions, those produced locally would save the nation chunks of forex.

If the sports agency is repackaged by independent bodies, the earnings from the sector would increase within a short space of time. The review of the structures is another way of enhancing revenues. Refusal of the nation to churn out better policies that are run by the collaboration efforts of the private investors could lead to stagnant revenue. A good lesson from the advanced economy of the world is the strong institutions that doing oversight functions over the businesses. In the nation, everything that can add values to live is a business. The businesses are registered and therefore abide by the regulation of the control agencies in order to have zero tolerance to substandard product and unsatisfactory services. By this, new thinkers join the businesses.

CHAPTER TWO
OPPORTUNITIES FROM THE VALUE CHAINS

Numerous are the opportunities from the value chains to add values to the national economy. Value chains are based on the creativity and the visionary style of management of the owners of business. Many artisans that are poor are those who lack ability to create new things. They do not have the intellect to create new ideas to enhance the growth of business. All technical aspects of a business could be repackaged and rebranded in a way to attract bigger sales and more wealth. A hair salon owner could engage in mobile service, home service, costumiers at film village for thespians, easily introduce the making and the selling of hair accessories, training for students at tertiary institutions as part-time lecturer for the entrepreneurship development course for the students. They could run shows or partner with people in show business to enrich their purses. Most of the cosmetics making business would find it a right business to engage hair salon to continue to generate more income and profits for other expansion of businesses. With all the added value business listed, the wealth being generated would constantly increase.

In short, value added job is a function of creativity of the entrepreneurs and economic think tanks of the government writing and implementing the policies. In the light of the contents in the first chapters, one can say that limitless are the opportunities from the value chains from each identified sectors in any economy. What a person can do is now a function of the level of creativity, natural intelligence, exposure to other cultural values, level of understanding of terrains and what the people, business or institutions are urgently require or desire at a particular point in time among several others. In most cases, there is no need for huge capital to start making fortunes from the identified opportunities from the value chains. Without doubt, new values are added to the existing value chains from the point of view of the creative persons.

Someone itched to know my business plans by the ventures under my watch. I politely responded "On a line of business that I started some years ago, there are several interrelated businesses on the pipeline. And each of the businesses could have different diversifications till eternity. As a publisher, listed types of books for different segmented buyers at segmented markets at the peak periods are to be published in different forms that would suit different segments of buyers at all locations by their status and tastes. We would produce high-cost printed books with the top grade materials for the top-notched people who could afford the prices and the low-cost material for students from low average homes. After this, I intended to run distinct brands of bookshops, conventional, mobile and online bookshops publishing different formats of books. Within the traditional bookshops at strategic locations such as schools, parks, fuel stations, restaurants among other places where there are congestion of passers-by targeted to be buyers and lovers of books, I had the intention to run library services within the conventional bookstores. The strategy is searching for the recommended books from the states ministry of education for the franchising business with the owners. I shall enter exchange programme of our globally rated books with reputable publishing business abroad. This does not stop my own publishing firm to bid with the books at the ministries and institutions that can recommend the books for the students across the nation. Each of the business affiliates has distinct selling and marketing strategies to grow the wealth with ease. In order to catch the interests of those who prefer audio-books shall have audio books. In addition, some of the books shall be reproduced into films, documentaries and reproduced in series.

A close pal in Information and communication technology chooses to run seminars and training programme instead of exhausting his resources in the production of software alone. Tutorials are done for the team (employees under his business payroll) in the office to produce certain software for target users while his training and consultancy department is on organizing trainings across the length and breadth of the nation and beyond. This is a product of marketing research department of his business. The analytical research findings showed numerous areas and how the business could earn more money as profits for the company. The business started collaboration with different institutions, publishing firms to reproduce their books as e-books and running their websites add greater values to his exposure and ability to earn more money as facilitator and instructor in the training being organized by both partners. He is earning money from the software, training, consultancy and partnering with publishing firms on hourly basis. This reminds me of a son of a billionaire that was said to be making more from ICT than what his father was earning from his chains of businesses across the land.

Referencing to the world gurus in all businesses, they have their hands in all businesses that have global value. The brands like Virgin of Sir Richard Branson, the businesses of Mark Zuckerberg, the new innovations of Jeff, the chief executive Officers of amazon.com among others confirmed the need for increasing the chains of businesses in order to increase the streams of making money. Many bestselling authors in the world are from different specializations. Many are lawyers, journalists, researchers, motivational speakers, politicians and business managers.

Visit fuel stations especially those located at strategic places, one would count number of businesses that are perfectly operated in a single premise. Many fuel stations are mini eatery, mini bookshop, mini confectionery shop, mini car washing, mini auto parts shop, lubricant shops, mini supermarkets for wines, juice, table-water, cards, flowers among others, mini lube for wheel balancing and fixing of auto parts. Many owners have installed facilities that would ensure visitors spend quality time for the products and services to be patronized within the station. At the end of the day, several products and services become sources of making money for the station.

An estate manager and property consultant could boost his or her income with either backward or forward integration. Imagine owning block making industry for the use of the repairs of houses under his or her custody. Such could also become builder of new cities by conversion of slums into befitting homes. The manager of estates could invest in the building of comfort stations and malls for rent and lease.

A business owner running frozen chicken shop could create space for the making of iced block in a commercial quantity for more money. The selling of cold juice, bottled water and the likes with the iced blocks in a container within the shop would add to the profits for the shop. This is the conversion of a shop into multi-shop.

In a firm is another firm at least. When the logistic and transportation of goods are costly. Common sense guides the firm owners to embrace launching and running transport sections and the outsourced job becomes part of the business.

The firm commercialize the section and the income is no more one but two. The public relation of a business that is being done by an independent office could be relocated within the premises. The quality publicist office could consult for others for a charging fee.

In the advanced economies especially for the business gurus, most of the income revolves within. They have cleaning services such as laundry and fumigating services. Transportation, clinic and other services could be run under the same brand. The international and wealthy Richard Branson of the Virgin business comes to mind. From the recording studio to recording company and several other jobs across all sectors all over the continents shown a man who is a master of how to keep adding value to the wealth of his.

During the lifetime of Nigerian business mogul, he owned concord group of companies such as concord group of newspapers, concord airline among others under the brand. He had other businesses that are of different brands as trademarks too across sectors. Like him, Alinko Dangote is having the brand in all the sectors thereby increasing his wealth every day. Think of any sector, Dangote is a household name. He is into manufacturing, processing, packaging, oil and gas, telecommunication among others. There is hardly a home, an institution or government circle where one or two products of Dangote is not patronized. The housewives and the chefs cannot do without the use of his salt, sugar, pasta, noodles, flour, juice etc and the structural or civil engineers cannot do without his cement. The shares of the listed companies in the Nigerian stock exchange keeps rising by the day. In the recent, one of the companies had gains of over one and ninety billion naira and the share of a product in a day was in billions of naira. Yet, the president of the company is working day and night to embrace the diversification into agriculture of the ruling administration from the investments on his area of interests- planting and processing of rice, wheat and other staple foods at a time he is massively investing on the biggest oil refinery in the continent of Africa. Would his income grow or otherwise?

Many institutions are running at financial loss simply because they do not enjoy huge patronage. Advertisements of the media institution monitored showed that they are dwindling as a result of the poor patronage of the goods and services of the industrial and service sectors. Had the sectors enjoy anticipated patronage by the clients, all other sectors would be beneficiaries from recycling of income in distribution of wealth. I suggest the collaboration efforts by different companies to enjoy huge patronage. Let us look at some instances. Let media station partner with the publishing company to promote books through serialization on an agreement on the sharing of profit. It is like 'I have the broadcasting platform and you have the product or service to sell, let's partner to have gains'. Abroad, there are publishing institutions that run media stations in order to focus on reaching buyers of their products across the world. The film makers and the media including the cinema and those in hospitality business could partner to improve on their earnings. With collaboration, all businesses and individuals with talents and skills to sell could become wealthy at their own pace.

Nigeria's duo of Fola T. Adeola and another colleague, Tayo O. by reports, started one of the greatest and fast expanding banks in Nigeria, Guaranty Trust Bank. After serving his terms as the chief executive office, he faced other challenges in telecoms business and other investments in finance world. Go deep in search for the number of companies he is a director or shareholder, they are in numbers. One would ask self 'would his wealth keep increasing or otherwise?'

In view of the above narratives, what is expected of a retired principal of a school? During his working days, he had no other source of earning than the monthly salary and the allowances. The retiree benefits are the pension after the collection of the gratuity. Let us assume that he had built a house, a three bedroom flat, from his salaries and allowances while in the service. At the period of retirement, his bones and body are too feeble to engage in any hectic job even his area of specialization-managing schools. His children had not started money earning jobs and therefore are dependents of his pension that is delayed in payment. What kind of growth would this person have in wealth? Of course, no grow of wealth but diminishing returns. This scenario is different from many teachers who had authored several books while in school from their leisure and research done within the free periods. By the time they retired from services, they might have series of books written and published. What comes from the editions of the works after leaving teaching service? Of course, royalties would be a right for the teachers adding as the supplement to the pension. If the pension per month is 10,000 and the total royalties from all the books per month is 20,000, then not less than 30,000 every month is enough to bootstrap and increasing the wealth day in day out. I could recall vividly that I started building my business interests from writing prose to sell for the established publishers. The joy of having the buyers spurred me into writing more on different issues. With the livelier spirits that the art of writing could be a right source of earning, publishing idea entered. At outset, I saw the new job as a capital intensive job just like any other jobs. I tried to reduce the process down to steps. Step one is to write and type on choice topics that would be acceptable by the target audience. With this in mind, several topics were writing upon. Step two is to engage in thorough editing and proof reading to identify avoidable errors. Step three is to present the work to outsiders to re-edit and criticize. Step four is to choose or decide whether to go self-publishing or give the script out to the traditional publishers at an agreed service charge by number of the copies produced. Along the line, a decision of self-publishing was adopted. I produced about 35 page book. Through hawking to school with the connections of admirers, enough revenues generated from the sales of the first book was invested on the second book which was the volume two of the first. The two series became inseparable pairs for schools after the release and the journey of self-publishing had started. In the resources ventures later registered with the corporate affairs commission, there are series of materials for all kinds of readers ranging from school materials to general public on different topics. All the books proffered solutions to challenges of life at all institutions, nations and individuals. Some of the materials were sent abroad for publishers to produce and promote. Within the few months of the release the books that solved employment crises across the nations, the books become popular and are at renowned libraries in the world with over 83% audience level by the reports of worldcat.org. Now, think about the anticipated royalties from all corners, within and outside the shores in different currencies, one can rightly say that the income would continue to soar.

Some books are recently released on my website showing how the proprietors of private schools could overcome the challenges facing the smooth running of their private businesses that lacked the supports of the government. One of the major challenges is the funding. In the book, not less than 13 ways were listed and concisely illustrated to solve the challenge. Now, how many jobs can this type of books created and how much in revenue can be made from the use of the content? Let me give some. Seminars and workshops could be organized by the use of the solutions proffered. Trainings at different periods could be held at negotiable charges for the stakeholders. New instructional materials could be produced and sold with the brand training and seminars. The other challenges solved in the books could also be sources of making more money. The end-products could become a source of raising several other big businesses like consultancy, counselling, publishing, marketing, branding and promotion of materials. And all of these are sources of generating revenues to the coffers of the owner. Would the earnings keep soaring or diminishing? It is a fact to repeat the mantra 'get wealthy by your own way or get poor by your own way'.

A bookshop owner referenced to in the book '**Creating new jobs from the existing jobs**' who decided to close shop for low profits as a result of low sales. The business advice to those in his shoes to create more income rather than closing shop. Numerous are opportunities to shore up the income from forward and backward integrations. Such could become publisher starting from children instructional materials that would be marketed and distributed by his bookshop. Mini library could be created within the bookshop and creating borrowing of books especially the stocks that are old but very popular. Writers can be attracted to bring their manuscripts for publishing on the basis of agreement. By all these channels and introduction of mobile bookshops or home-delivery strategy of distribution of books to segmented buyers such as other bookshops, libraries, institutions, agencies and people in the high offices who could not afford to shop for books and materials at bookshops. A bookstore owner that engages in franchise could make more money. Imagine the income of a bookshop that entered franchise with a popular retailing firm like amazon.com with the advert amazon bookstore in his or her nation. The brand name would automatically attract huge patronage and the income shores up within a short space of time.

Many a company that is into road and building constructions in Nigeria today have their quarry instead of depending on the supplies of the private quarry business owners. During the initial stage when they do not have right to own quarry, the private owners milked them dry with inflated prices. The control over the supplies from their sites have reduced or normalized the charges from the private owners if there is need for more supplies that are urgent. At outset, many builders used to depend on the private owners of machine to use at site. The calculation in a year runs to millions and the decision to own theirs today has saved the firms millions. They also make money from renting the machine out for other engineering companies at good service charge.

When I was working in a newspaper company. Several things were of interest in the style of management. Instead of travelling with the papers being supplied to all corners of the world with the company's vehicle, the management prefer to engage courier service and some of the companies that used to travel wide to cut costs in maintenance service of the vehicles. It was very cheap to send them than the burning of costly fuels and payments for all tolls, wear and tear of the vehicles not to talk of the risks and remuneration of as many drivers put on the road as possible. Another thing is that, through time management, editions of the works were produced at different times within the premises. Lastly, many independent publishers used to come to the firm for publishing of their works as they could not afford the machines for the job. Mostly, they were publishers with no printing machine! In the company, only the printing charge was paid for as they used to come with the print material especially the mill. The most interesting thing was that the publishers were into the production of series of journals under their brand business name. In a nutshell, if the daily morning paper is not bringing the right income, the evening papers would do; if the breaking newspapers do not, the sports papers would, if the weekly papers do not, the monthly magazine would do. Many newspapers are into award presentations and public speaking business to earn more recognition and money for the business. Politicians are now the major patron of the newspapers especially the journalists. The writings of the men of the pen, just like the history writers, end a regime and install another administration. The unnecessary and false whistle blowing of issues by journalists and broadcasters through their pens and mouths respectively beyond imagination could catalyze wars in nation and turn the nation into a stage of war.(Read more in the book '**Words are absolutely powerful**' by the same author)

Getting more wealth is an ability to reduce cost by introducing measures and inputs that would enhance this to become a reality. As the expenses go south, the revenues would increase and such could be used for either forward or backward diversification. The reverse is the case for the poor. The poor would get poorer if the expenses keep increasing as the income is stable or lower. Is this not a good reason for the condensation of the topic- growing wealthy or poor a choice by one's desire?

Each time I heard about the insurance firm employees, particularly the marketers, inability to create new customers and even getting target premiums. How much of the acts that established the insurance business are used to the letter? Had insurance acts followed the areas covered as specified, insurance firms have the advantage to generate more income or grow the wealth of the companies or the sector.

Nations that do not have right (stable) budget at least a surplus one would risk running into liquidation and social insecurity from the scourge of unemployment breeding vicious acts. Deficit budget, when the chance of getting the target money, is unpredictable and uncertain (not cocksure) could mean higher poverty in the land. It is applicable to individuals, offices homes and business institutions. It is wrong to run deficit budget. It is right to run a budget on the basis of the available financial resources at hand. By doing the former, the hope rises and if the raise hope is not met by expectation, the poor becomes poorer. In the latter, there is no raise of spirit and there could be stability on the land when wealth could be created the more by initiatives of the individuals and the institutions.

As a writer, I can boost my income and royalties by writing about celebrated brands in individuals, institutions, companies and governments for good returns. Call such ghost writers if you desire. Yes, a ghost writer of my shoes is one that would unveil the right facts about such target to present the right information that are never libelous. From the launchings and the serial presentations, more recognitions would be attained for the countless people who would engage me in faction stories about their lives too. In the book '**Creating new jobs from the existing jobs**' from the author, it is clear as snow that numerous are the new jobs that are creatable from just one job. Do you know that the ghost writing could bring about media-based jobs? Do you know the number of the value chains jobs that are created from the films and documentaries productions of the subject written about by the ghost writer? When I see a nagging thespian on the basis of poor remuneration from the producers, I frowned. I have my reasons. Every actor and actress has the ability to script and produce books and films too. They had the right and the skills based on their field experience to produce their own films. They could market and distribute their works effectively and generate huge income. We have illustrated how writers of films can independent producers even with zero capital in the volume one of the popular book 'Jobs with zero capital. A thespian could boost his earning from collaboration efforts with those in the fashion and leisure including hospitality industries. They are like talented football or sportsmen of repute whose endorsements of products as the faces of the institutions could be a right channel of generating additional income to what is being earned as actor or actresses. In this clime, many notable actresses have also diversified to become costume sellers, costumiers, body accessories distributors, make-up artists, stage thespian, motivational speakers, comediennes, reality shows facilitator and producers, event planners, concert repertoire and singers. Their popularity in the profession of choice has turned them with men with Midas touch. In addition to the list of jobs, they could run broadcasting-based jobs, write columns and feature writers for newspapers and magazines for a price, author books and be publicists for institutions and governments. If wide spread of 'hate song' by a popular artiste could be said to be one of the negative contributors which catalyzed the inter-tribal wars between Hutus and Tutsis in Rwanda, then love-based songs, love-focused films, balanced documentaries and features from the thespians could be good sources of earning big. In the international jobs of meddling into disputes, they could churn out works that would be used to douse tensions in nations and by so doing increase the sources of earning. In Nigeria, the rich thespians and singers are those that are into cross over jobs. The artistes could effectively sing in all major languages and English. The thespians could fit in to the local films and English-speaking films simply because of their fluency in all the dialects like the original or indigenous speakers. An actor with this gift of crossing over is always an attraction to be face of the brands. Such earns as ambassador to big-earning companies. If a writer, a broadcaster, an analyst, a critic, an accountant, a lawyer and all aspects of profession is multilingual, the chance of earning more money than his comrades is very high. Politicians that can speak several dialects have the best chance of being elected into offices or serve as the right representatives as diplomat, ambassador and spokespersons for the nation all over the world. In the business world, a business institution that has multilingual marketers would generate and keep increasing the degree of profits making for the companies. It is easy for such to sell franchise to other big investing partners. Banks would prefer to support such business institutions that are blessed with such multilingual employees or team in the administration and departments.

It is not a good business for a business that has market challenge of the competitors and failing to proffer solutions to meet and subdue the challenges. Every business is a challenge to others vice versa. The competition challenge would not allow business to rest but to plan and strategize on how to boost sales. If a business is located within the congestion of population that have a very high chance of loving the product, then little efforts shall be expended to generate huge sales and shore up the profits. A seller of beverages who has space to contain or host people could move up to have eatery within the premises. It is better if the publishing company, a private library or at least a private bookstore is located within a school or very close to the school. Government would save a lot of money to have the industries at the areas where the raw materials are found in commercial quantities instead of using huge resources to transport such materials to the processing company elsewhere. The saved accumulation is a wealth for the nation as the cost of production shall go south. A product can be produced and sold at over 1000 miles away from the factory. It is a good business plan for a business to have thoroughly criticize market information before the resumption for production. A business must not release into the market such products that people would not buy. 'What is makeable is what is saleable' from the common economic parlance. Make what they would buy. If a business does otherwise, it will continue to record low or no sale. This is how a business gets poor as choice. A business that is working on how to get more wealth by its choice is the one that has created awareness and customers as a pre-production activities. In some cases, there may have been pre-deal of demanded supplies from the customers before the product arrives the markets and malls.

Those big businesses that are crumbled like a pack of cards fail simply because they fail to identify endless value chains or the value added jobs of the business. It is puzzled for international business to crash in the face of market environment challenges. It is expected that such companies might have learnt so much in the markets across the world. It is easy for such to withstand the unhealthy competitions withier garnered market situation experience that must have been applied to the letter. We have done justice on how firms can generate huge sales and profits in the published book **"Winning huge sales and increasing clients base"** from the same author.

In the history of Nigeria, Malaysia came to pick some palm kernel nuts for large scale farming of oil palm in the nation. With massive gains from this venture, every other sector start to develop. Today, the nation is one of the richest in that part of Asia. It is developing faster than Nigeria that has lots of resources that are left idle. What are my dragging at? The potentials are high for nations to develop a sector first before investing the gains to develop others like the Asian nation. Develop the education sector. Introduce vocational and artisanal jobs to the courses after reforming the curriculum towards producing self-reliance students from all schools. With this in place and supports of the right materials and inputs, the development of the nation has started and the wealth creation would be as easy as a, b c.

Nations in Africa are diversifying into the agricultural sector in order to generate both wealth and employment from the agricultural economy. By this, they would satisfactorily feed the mouths and the industries with foods and raw materials respectively. Good examples are Ethiopia and Rwanda in their development of apiculture, livestock production and horticultural economy. Some are into the development of the knowledge-based economy despite their progress in agricultural economy. A good example is Rwanda. One can imagine the biggest market in Africa, Nigeria if she can develop all the sectors at a swap as a result of the huge potentials to develop all to the maximum with the available resources. What huge wealth the nation shall generate within a short space of time!

The nation just as individual and institutions can boost their earnings from the knowledge-based economy if the potential and the resources are put into maximum use. Without mincemeat of words, outside natural disasters, individual, institutions and the nations that are wallowing in poverty choose to be poor!

Nigeria has huge potentials to be financially independent in such sectors like tourism, sports, knowledge-based economy not to talk of agricultural economy, mining sector and others.

CHAPTER THREE
GETTING WEALTHY YOUR OWN WAY

Getting rich or poor, by persons, institutions and the nations, is a choice, I repeat. We have supported this in the previous chapters. Attitude pays a major role in the making and growing of wealth. Attitude to develop ideas and write policies matters. Loss of efficiency and effectiveness in addition to patriotism for the nation has cost many nations huge direct foreign investors. Recently, the International Oil Companies (IOCs) in oil deposit areas had to relocate in droves as a result of incessant kidnapping for ransom and general insecurity from the militant groups. Nations that were making fortunes from tourism have become low earner from the sector as a result escalating terrorism and other forms of insecurities on the nation. I had seen several once-thriving businesses that had closed shops and factories simply because they failed to adopt the style of promotion and selling strategies of the time. Simple decisions to dish out the modern approaches to management are enough to ensure continual growth of businesses hence the wealth vice versa. Security of lives and property is major contributor to the wealth continual growth.

I came across a school proprietor who was sharing the challenges facing school business generally. One of them is funding as a result of inability of majority of the parents to pay school charges in full. It simply means that the schools are having lower income by the day instead of using the resources at their beck and call to make more money. He added that his visit to big schools showed that they had very low enrolment and a few students in attendance. 'The two challenges have practicable solutions. Each school has not less than ten ways to grow their incomes' (details in one of my books '**School business: challenges, solutions and prospects**'). I quickly reminded him of one of the solutions where schools should produce reading and instructional-based books and materials for the pupils at the pre-nursery, nursery to primary one classes. After this reply, he bared his mind on one of those challenges facing such interest which is distribution to make sales at the right time to avoid tying down the capital invested. 'This is when school should constantly develop distribution strategies that suit the environment where the business is located. You drop after exhausting such for another to come on board. Schools where such is done could introduce exchange programme where there is interchange of books or such materials. All nations that are getting poorer by the day is through the bad attitude to governance. Many leaders are square pegs in a round hole. Attitude to administration of leaders could easily grow the wealth of the nation. Let me quickly use instances of two nations. Singapore and Nigeria had different leaders at different times and periods in the histories of the nations. In the former, he recognized corruption as a bane to national growth and development and he worked selflessly with positive attitudes to stamp out the scourge. Today, the nation moved away from third world to the first world.

In the latter, there was a government whose leader at the time of oil boom was reported to have said 'our problem is not money but what we would use the money for'. He set up a committee and cash was recommended to be paid to civil servants and those in powers instead of developing road map to turn the nation into a first world nation from the third world like the Singaporean visionary leader by investing in all infrastructures and researches that would transform the nation to the path of positive growth. This is our final conclusion from the researches into works and even the Divine scriptures. Being poor in money does not mean poor in other resources like physical strength, natural intelligence, wisdom, brilliance, skill and talents.

A nation does not need more than security of investment to grow more wealth in some nations. One may have little at outset, his art of saving from little gains and interest in investing the little would grow the income and wealth with time. Many who have a skill never bother to acquire other skills. Many who have a certificate does not deem it fit to seek knowledge in others to add to their knowledge. Who knows whether the new skills, information, knowledge, certificate, connection, affiliation and pothers would be the prerequisites to grow the wealth at hand?

In view of the above, he who desires to grow his wealth must imbibe the right attitudes to saving, learning new things (skills, knowledge, talents of others, latest information in vogue..) through self-development by attending seminars, read books, watch documentaries, films, analyse news, engage in research, adopt the works of research, use the latest technologies, drop certain old habits and change his attitudes to the negatives.

Individuals could nurture a viable seed to grow wealth and they in some cases spearhead how to create and grow the wealth either of a business or the nation. The builders of the modern Rome did not build the edifice in a day as shown in the common maxim '<u>to be a man is not a day job, besides Rome is not built in a day</u>'. Wealth starts to grow from zero-dollar. Capital-intensive jobs have sources from zero-capital (Read details inside '**Jobs with zero-capital vol. Two** from the same author). Constant drops of water makes an ocean. Every wisely invested time, money, and other resources grow to become ocean of wealth. I had lived with a guy who used to work for two days in week. He used to say that he did not like to work till he exhausted the last penny earned from the two-day job. How would this kind of person grow wealthy in life? He did not value the art of saving for future uses especially turning round the money to start growing his wealth. I have seen several business owners whose businesses suddenly dropped in sales and incomes who decided to sell off the businesses. This is a wrong step. The new jobs they are thinking of investing upon would also face certain challenges later. Why don't they fix the problem and find practicable solutions to the challenges facing such once-thriving business? '<u>A known devil is better than an unknown angel</u>' as a proverb says.

A business that an owner knows its pro's and con's should not be abandoned for another new trade overnight especially trades in vogue. The proverbial '<u>Jack of all trades is a master of none</u>'. Man learns on the job at hand. Investment grows with the challenges of time and places. He should learn about the business before he starts developing interests and investing in such business. A good business owner or manager is someone who fixes the problem when it occurs. Actors do not run away from wars. It is either he's a victor or died a hero or martyr. It takes a courageous to win and woo wealth to his side. Prudency and financial discipline on what to invest on and how to allocate resources would combine to grow wealth of individual, institutions and the nations. 'Winners would never quit and quitters would never win' as a maxim goes. There is no big deal for a business to be sold to another investor who has better way to manage such kind of business. Some even build a business at the right location, operate for some times to enhance the goodwill before selling such business at a very big price. Yes, this is an idea to grow one' capital. The estate managers used to build malls, houses and the likes for sale. They buy dilapidated structures at the right commercial places, restructure and them and resell at high prices to grow their wealth. But for a man in business, it looks odd for a school proprietor for instance to sell the school for simple reason of low enrolment or challenges such as funding, low income among others. There are solutions to those challenges.

In retrospect, attitudes could make or mar a progress in the wealth generation and grow. What is expected of an individual who refuses to acquire more certificates or skills when that is the new prerequisites to aspire for a position of authority? Such would continue to be stagnant and wallowing in poverty. While his mates who have acquired the necessary or meet the requirements are promoted to the new ranks, such remains in the same position till his retirement from service. Individuals who prefer to spend their earning or disposable income heavily on the essential needs without investing in the future like on acquiring of education, latest skills and knowledge in information and communication technology among others would grow to become poor. This applies to the nations also. There must be genuine interest in investing for the future. Each time my spouse discussed the poor state of Nigeria especially in terms of economy and politics in particular, I used to tell her that the problem should not be piled up on the present crop of leaders but what the past leaders had planted in bad seeds of economy and ethno-religion based and bitter politics. The corrupt people in government are following the footsteps of the founding fathers. Most of the founding fathers, by studies and revelations, owned estates here and abroad and their children went to exotic schools unlike the children of the masses. They selected friends and concubines to manage political offices and enjoyed the paraphernalia of offices which they keep improving upon at the expense of the people.

In fact, when a former leader assumed the position again, he monetized the public offices which skyrocketed the art of looting. Where did the leaders now and then acquire such stupendous wealth if not from the nation they had looted? The simple supportive analogy is the tree crops. Those who planted them never live to eat from the fruits but the latter generation. The economic downturn the nation is experience today is as a result of bad governance of the past. It is easy to destroy than to build. Is this not enough for the calls for restructuring of such nation in all aspects of life?

As aforesaid, the attitudes of leaders, at homes, in private and public institutions, at the helms play the style and pace of growth in wealth of such nation. Such attitudes include the financial discipline. If the leaders fail to prioritize the needs but blindly spend on frivolities, this attitude depletes the nation' resources. In some other nations, the type of security needed is financial security where the financial institutions are capable to support the intellectual capital to grow the wealth of the nation. In some cases, the physical security against social vices that could drive away investors must be the priority. The lifestyle of the people used to render them poor. Most value number of children they cannot fend for especially in a nation whose political ideology does not provide free education and health care services. The expenses on the basic needs would continue to eat deep into the finance of such families as the children grow in age. Nations also remain poor for failure to use the statistics to plan on the people. The nations that are advancing in all the sectors of the economy cannot play with the statistics that are churned out at interval. In the case of business institutions, the need to place the priority could be a decision that would boost the wealth.

It is apparently incredible for educational institutions especially the tertiary institutions like the universities, the polytechnics, the mono-technics and even the technical and vocational schools to be financially dependent on the government like the health care institutions. Each of them should be earning big from the productions of the students who are trained to appreciate their intellectual property and natural skills. Many institutions in the advanced economies are run like private businesses where several materials are converted into wealth of great values. A good example is the development of the sports to the level of producing quality athletes. Some sports are owned by the school as assets and commercial ventures. Schools could produce materials of students for sale on the school portal or specially created e-library owned and managed by the school. Imagine the earnings of Oxford Press for Oxford University. In America, some universities have basketball teams in the National Basketball Association league or contests to win prizes and prices in huge forex to the coffers of the schools. The leaders at different points in time determine the rate of growth of wealth. The prodigal one could squander the wealth while a right person who is selfless would continue to grow the wealth by applying the right attitudes to governance or the position of leaderships at any level no matter the whisperings of the evils who are the sycophants at the corridors of authority and power.

In the business parlance, the choice of branding, advertisements, marketing, promotion, the style of managerial of the staff among others could play major role in the growing of the wealth of the companies or otherwise. It is expected that the business that has dwindling patronage to develop new strategies to boost income and maintain growth. A business in financial downturn due to low or no patronage should constantly devise new selling and distribution strategies. These could take different dimensions and sizes as the dynamics of the business environment demand. In a nation where information and Communication Technology has reduced physical shopping of the target clients or customers, the business should develop online shops to reach out to the customers. In fact, the online shop is a good source of generating more customers in several millions across the nations provided there is perfect channel of distribution of the product or quality delivery of services. With this, the wealth of the company would geometrically improve. Many businesses in comatose may have to change the advertisement slogans or use the new faces as ambassadors of the company products or services.

In the light of the above, we shall look at how attitudes could grow wealth of individuals, the businesses and the nation at outset before churning out of jobs one can engage on to improve the wealth.

THE ATTITUDES TO SAVING

An art of saving should be imbibed to grow the wealth. It is bad to spend above the means. If the income after tax of an institution is 50 million, the institution must not budget on 100 million especially if the interest rate and conditions of loan are unavoidable. A poor man that pretends to be rich is not loved by Almighty Creator according to the saying of the noblest. Never should a poor arrogantly appear to be rich. Cut your coat according to the piece of cloth and not your size as you may have big frame that outweighs the yards of cloth. Students who are prudent in spending would have enough to invest on money-earning ventures within and outside the school premises. Many companies that outsource certain jobs may be able to conserve money. We can look at the instances of paying 10 million naira for transportation for all workers in a year compare to having a bus for the staff. If a bus cost 5 million naira and the cost of servicing and fuels in a year is 3 million naira. 2 million naira is saved for other viable business use to earn more profits.

THE ATTITUDES TO SELF-RESTRICT (MORAL DISCIPLINE)

Ability to have control over one's spending right is a restraint is a good way to enrich the wealth. Restrain your tongue from hate speeches to avoid losing patronage of your goods and services. Refrain from spending extravagantly. Imbibe the art of right investing on investments to grow the wealth. Kindness and generousity could boost popularity to earn contracts. Good leaders are appointed on the basis of good character and quality ability to serve well. By this, such entrusted with public post has grown his credibility in the nations. Through the assumption of offices for occupying the positions of trust, the leaders have been rebranded from nobody to somebody of huge substance and value to all. These leaders earn from writing books and public speaking after leaving the office. A good example is in the former President from an advanced nation.

THE ATTITUDE TO ALLURING THINGS

Studies show that people allure good things of life and even compete in the procurement. Institutions used to have dressing code that may be parasitic to the earning of the staff. Men love beautiful ladies. Beautiful ladies love costly body accessories. She has tastes for imported materials in fabrics and designs in shoes and clothes. She loves to eat the best and branded foods and drinks. She desires to live in mansions very huge to maintain. She likes to ride in exotic cars at costly maintenance cost. All these alluring materials are tempting to commit crimes and deplete the income of the providers. Business institutions used to brand their companies by their pretence to be rich as they used to acquire fleet of exotic cars for their senior staff, sponsoring them abroad for training instead of doing such within aside the list of paraphernalia of offices and their aesthetics. Today, there are architectural design offices of many notable financial institutions that had run bankrupt and liquidated in Nigeria most probably as a result of funds mismanagement by wrong attitudes in the business corporate decision. Yes, there is no big deal to satisfy one's desire but not above the means. It is right to spend as it is bad to miser. It is sensible to have taste for good things but excessive consumption or addiction could render one poor. Many who buy within the disposable income speculated or earmarked for consumption and the other earning for investment and speculative investment purpose would usually grow the wealth. A man should avoid spending much on obsolete, second-hand or fairly used assets that would gulp money for repair but those ones that would boost income. Procurement of assets that do not have spare parts owing to the release of latest assets of modern technology is a wrong investment. Assets that would not generate immediate income is tantamount to tying down capital for a while. Such assets include landed property, rentable apartment, commercial vehicles and rentable machines among others. Acquiring fleet of cars under tarpaulin, houses with no apartments for rent, fallow land growing grass or weeds that are not leased out for commercial purposes. One does not need to buy smartphones that are used for selfies and not for commercial use.

THE PERSONAL EGO AND ETHNO-RELIGION INFLUENCE

Individual and institutions, not to talk of government, could grow the wealth or otherwise if ego and bias on the basis of ethno-religion influence. If the right person is appointed to manage a position as a trust, the position would boost the wealth vice versa. In management, it is not 'this is how I want it'. This is being bossy and dictatorial by the leader. 'Two good heads, they say, are better than one' according to a proverb. A good leader should seek and share opinions of others. They must have due respect for what others have in views. All counter opinions and views would end up to bring about the best decision as the final conclusion. This is the reason for having round tables in the conference rooms at institutions. The breadwinner must have time for discussions on the sources and allocations of income at home. If the decision is to expand the source, the path to tread is discussed and right steps taken shall boost the income for the family. At the level of business institutions, the discussion on the challenges facing the institutions at the round table would keep improving the income and wealth of the companies. A nation whose people in the positions of authority does not periodically meet to discuss the prevalent issues affecting the income being generated and its distribution would be stagnant in the comity of nations. Nations that are not growing are mostly those that do not allow critics contributions. No man can claim to be 'Mr. Fountain of knowledge' or 'an island'. No single tree could make a forest as the maxim says. Views of others must be sought and respected. A family man invested on two buildings at miles apart at time simply because his business was boosting. He failed to finish one structure before embarking on another. He was like someone investing at the same time on two different businesses or a nation that embarks on different projects at the same time within the same fiscal year despite the limited resources to fund the project especially when the budget is running on deficit. The man ended up abandoned the two structures at advanced stages. He lost his source of income when patronage of his business dwindled sharply. Many businesses that ended half-way and the chains of abandoned projects that scattered round the nation show that wrong decision in investments. Had the three faced a project at a time, the sum of capital at hand could be rightly invested on money-earning ventures after finishing the single project at a time.

What are the jobs that can boost the wealth to individuals, institutions and the nations?

START AS RAW MATERIAL PRODUCTION: PRODUCE LOCAL CONTENTS

Every business can use forward and backward integration approaches to shore up their wealth creation. This is a very simple thing. Apply your sense. A learned friend told me how he transformed himself from being an owner of a barbing salon to further his education as a result of discovering the brilliance in him. He was challenged by the events of the time. He thought of the income being earned at the moment. Even though, his earning was enough to sustain his needs. Would the amount be enough to sustain a family when he gets married? Would he be able to feed his aging parents and siblings that are dependents on him? Suffice the reason for the dusting of his ordinary level certificate to pay for joint admission and matriculation board examination. He passed and met the cut-off point for law. The rest is history. Today, his source of income has become huge. He earns respect as one of the men of the silk. A brief for a client within the comfort of his law office could earn him today what a 30-day barbing service would never bring in income.

Every person must think over the income to sustain self and dependents. Every business institution must grow its profits to meet the financial challenges, diversification and expand the tentacles of business. Governments must design wealth-creation enhancing policies in all departments. What does your business need to improve sales in complementary or supplementary product or service? What can promote your product or service? What are the inputs needed to produce your goods or services? Can you produce any of these? If you can, then you have created new line of goods or services in order to start increasing the wealth of your firm. A publisher is known with unique ways of promoting their products with the company-owned media station. Imagine the huge potential customers that would be created if such publisher has television and radio stations where serialization of the books and other printed materials are marketed.

Saying it as it is, I was lured into submitting my material for publishing in a company abroad simply because of the television station where the books are done justice with to promote and attract sales. This station shall surely be a channel for promotion of other products such as the books converted into films and documentaries. The featuring of the authors, the thespians, the film producers among others would attract placement of advertisements from all other sectors like the fashion world, music, arts and entertainment among others. There would be attractions of adverts just like aesthetic stadium of popular and adequately branded football teams in a well-packaged leagues of the world for different sports. A team can boost their income from partnering with sport kits companies and insurance for the crew. In the popular English Premiership, sponsors are from all corners and thereby increasing the wealth of the club. The level of thinking shall play major role in the additional wealth creation. Through the flexibility of the rules of games, it is possible for star athletes and sportsmen to participate in films at a price for the persons and the team they are under contracts with. In the public outdoor electronic billboards are endorsements of the popular players from popular teams from the popular leagues of the world to increase the incomes of the teams. One can see that there are limitless ways on the way to shore up the income of individuals, institutions and governments. Cogitate!

Along the streets are electronic billboards from the outdoor advertising companies that are always empty. Empty simply because they are patronized. I used to monitor the radio and television stations that play music more than releasing jingles and video shots of promotion of goods and services. The management lacks the skills to attract advertisements from the companies, institutions and individuals. In the book, '**Winning huge sales and increasing clients base**' by the same author, we identify several ways for the media-based stations to grow their incomes. For the benefit of this theme, media stations should develop new concepts in programmes and documentaries that would attract larger audience listening and watching the stations. Many mistakenly promote their popularity through old films when most target clients like sports especially football. Freebies could add more value to the level of patronage. Collaboration of the management with the promoters of entertainment, fashion, sports federation and their contests, government institutions and agencies towards sensitization of the public of the government activities would boost the growth of wealth of the sector practitioners.

From studies, I know of a school proprietor that started with extra mural class at good location. Later, it introduced some courses to Cambridge, TOEFL, advanced certificates and others. Today, it has developed new businesses in virtual learning or e-learning where classless school or mobile school is in operation for special categories of students that can afford the fees. It also runs a centre in a well-equipped ICT section hall with all the relevant aesthetics where Computer-Based Tests (CBT), for university admission of universities within and outside the shores, is taking place at a charge from the body coordinating the admission examinations into tertiary institutions. One could see the education business that started with coaching centre has grown to become affiliates of universities within and abroad in addition to partnership with examination bodies and institutes. How creative the proprietor of the school in making more wealth by the day. We can classify all the innovations as the production of local contents to expand the business in order to boost the wealth of the business.

In view of the above, local contents production by government agencies and departments including the institutions under the tiers of government is a way of increasing the revenue base of the nation. The flexible economic policy, supported by favourable political policy, is another means of making more revenues for the nation. The private licensing of institutions is another way of boosting the nation's economy revenue base. The nations used to have the local contents in the raw materials as a business policy that would promote wealthy creation and employment generation. The local content policy that targets the production of human and non-human resources has been a way to getting wealthy at one's way. Many years back, there are nations whose educational institutions are too strong that they produced manpower for many developing and underdeveloped nation. A good example is Cuba. Exports from some nations have been the raw mineral resources while to the buyers of the raw materials, the exports are the finished goods from the raw materials. The choices are with people seeking for wealth creation. During the periods of economic recession, all the sectors demanded for full implementation of the local contents policy. All investors at all sectors are to employ their manpower locally. Many expatriates from abroad lost their positions for the locally-trained professionals. The productions at factories embraced not less than 80% as local contents in the raw materials.

By this, employments were generated locally across the boards. And the demand in the markets for local contents got bigger. In order to meet the increasing demands, there were proliferation of businesses with added value chains. There were instances where people converted their fallow lands and spacious backyards into subsistence farms. Some deliberately procured landed property and locally-built machines to start small scale business of producing raw materials from firms aside the farms. Experiences garnered in the course have exposed the writer on endless ways to starting wealth at one's pace. In the files, a road traffic police officer on duty was relieved by another officer. We were discussing over supplements to earnings at the period of recession when prices of foods, goods and services are soaring by the day. He showed his palm. 'I am running a cassava powder factory within my compound. With just 50,000 naira, you could start the processing business and make a minimum of 8,000 naira per week. This is based on the calculated shared profits after the processing and sales to the wholesaler. This is when the market price is at 3,500 naira per measure (bath). If the wholesale price at the market, depending on the season rises to 3,600 or more, the gain increases. The wholesalers too would make their own money from the packs to about 200 per measure and 26 in each process making 5,200 from his narratives as market measures price. There is no way your capital will reduce but rather you make profit every week'. It was as if I was hearing this for the first time. So, 50,000 can yield 8,000 in a process per week. What of if 100,000 is invested, around 16,000 from the business per week. One can imagine having about 200,000 for the business on weekly basis, not less than 32,000 shall be the realizable profits and this gives a target of 1.536 million naira in a year!

As being emphasized, the target net profits in a year could be more than this if the market prices are at average of 3650 in the year. One can imagine if the trader move up to brand the garri as OYO BRAND, EGBA BRAND, IJEBU BRAND, IGBO BRAND etc. and such are bagged in transparent but highly aesthetic packs at different sizes and prices, the popularity of the product would cut across all races and the market acceptability increases. To increase the income, the seller could diversify into rebranding of more staple foods and sell to places near and far. The gains from the supplies could be used for backward diversification by the seller. Through this, the raw materials are produced for the processing and packaging firms. With this chain, the income keeps increasing for the proprietors of the business. It is easy for the repackaged company to increase the routes of supplies for the increased list of schools, malls, fuel stations, markets and engaging retailers and hawkers. In addition, a literate and export-driven trader would make internet search for the buyers abroad to earn forex from this activity. In the world today, migration has become a common venture, people move from place to place for different reasons. And many do not like to drop their cultural values for the new environment easily. Nigerians living abroad would like to have taste of Nigerian foods even once in a week. The suppliers of garri to all parts of the world where the nationalities are would enjoy huge sales and make his fortune.

A company consulted my office over writing a proposal to source for loan from a financial institution. It is apicultural company that has acquired two acres of land. A plot is being used to serve as test-run. In the financial analyzes from a year harvest on the basis of the market value of the major product, honey, 55.25% of the capital was the gross profit. The sales of the bee-wax, honey combs and the venoms added much to the gain from a plot. Imagine if such secure loan to increase the production in the remaining eleven plots of the two-acre land for the business! If the company could engage in international supplies, forex shall be obtained from the exports. Forward integration could lead the apicultural economy company into drug making, cosmetics among others. Each chain shall add to the income hence the wealth of the company.

A teacher under contract in a school, public or private, could improve his earning if he can offer post-school services such as mobile tutorial, virtual impartation of knowledge with his smartphone and social media handle especially specialized blog or personal website, selling of instructional materials online among others. Teachers are right products to be authors of books on their chosen specializations, actors and actresses of plays, orators, poets, journalists, seminar facilitators among others. I know of lecturers that are not just researchers, instructors but are consultants to big firms while in the tertiary institution. I counselled an unemployed guy to engage in part-time teaching job hence he can have excess time to create more income from grooming of talented stars from different fields based on his qualification as physical and health education course he studied at the university. Such teacher could be teacher-on-air if he has advanced his skill with information and communication technology with its innovations and apps. By these, wealth is created and distributed with ease.

ENGAGE IN BACKWARD INTEGRATION

Moving further, one who has laid his hands on forward integration could also engage in backward integration as an added value through financing farmers to produce large scale of cassava. The produce would boost the income of the farmers and increase the cassava output per annum. The other added values of the crop include starch-making, fufu, white flour and the animal feeds from the peeled barks of cassava. All of them can be packaged in way that they could be exported like garri. Ask me how each can be added more values to create jobs. Partnership with the vegetable farmers could work for the consumers. By this, consumers would buy cassava flour with vegetable, vegetable plus peppers and cassava flour. The merchant could partner with the processing factory who have the technical and machinery to produce starch in large scale. The same could be done for the production of cassava flour in large scale for the other users like the bakers. Several are the moves to ensure the forward integration for the business becomes a reality.

Each time I saw guys and damsels taking selfies with their phones, I used to think about the value chains of the type of phones they are carrying. Instead of free selfies, many would have taken special designs and save on phone for the international designers. It is shopping designs for them for a good fee. Naturally, there are limitless for snapshots. Creativity and the interests of the owners of the browsing mobile phones with free megabytes for all credit calls card procured.

TURN THE SLUMS INTO NEW CITIES

Estate managers add values to structures to make money. With partnering with financial institutions, many crumbling structures that are located at lucrative commercial outlets could be turned into highly-sought for structures for rent or lease. Search for the structures for sale or lease. Prepare attractive proposal to the financial institutions for funding. Both would be able to earn money from the partnership. The successful business moguls in the world are those in the three basic needs that have now become six with the addition of education, health care and security services. I am close to an estate managers who added values to a house he procured at 1.5 million with just around 500,000 naira and he later sold the rehabilitated structure at 2.6 million naira. All the deals done within three months. One can imagine the gains such could be making from the essential needs of all people.

MAKE THE MILLIONS FROM SELLING

Selling is the greatest avenue for individuals and corporate business institutions could amass wealth and keep growing it by the day. Ask about the foremost sellers among the retailers; the names of amazon.com, barnes and noble.com among others would come to the fore. The chief executive officers of one of this company is rated first among the richest in the world. There is no limit to the development of selling strategies for a business to use. The peculiarity and the dynamism of the operating business environment determines the selling strategies. For instance, studies show that the increasing number of licensed broadcasting media in the nation has limited the loyal audience of the stations. Also, the quality of audience does not cover the right targets to have knowledge about products and services that are marketed in the media. To sell in this type of environment, personal selling through door to door, office to office, public road selling and the selling outlets or stations at markets for selling through hawkers shall be the better option to improve on the earnings. In addition, there could be more sales with less stress and no logistic cost through the use of collaboration style of distributing and selling. Media houses, hotels, fuel stations and others could serve as the selling points for books and films including fashion designs and artworks provided the makers have entered business agreements with the stations. Without doubt, the internet facilities at affordable rate and the digital innovations in gadgets have helped the sellers to be foremost in the retailing and distribution business. Strategic ways can be adopted depending on the types of products that are put on sale by the prospective sellers. A greater method of earning big in selling is through franchising especially for a franchiser that has dynamic strategies for the location of the sales outlets and the distribution network of the product under the franchising agreement. Many franchise sellers have the potentials to start earning and growing wealthy provided right business decisions are churned out at the right time or as the market situations demand. Many phone sellers in the cities are running on franchise. Approach the brands you intend to sell. A guy was into selling of frozen chicken and turkey. He sought for assistance and was guided on how to enter franchise agreement with the available resources with him.

Wise students have converted their smartphones into mobile office and the service station where all their choice products and services are sold to prospective clients. Those who are bloggers are earning every day through their pinging on the phone. Ping to promote variants of products and services.

EMBRACE EXPORTING OF FARM PRODUCE

In the recent, the ministry of agriculture in Nigeria adopted exporting of yams and some other farm produce abroad. The policy at outset is a ticket for the farmers to increase their productions in farms in order to have excess for exportation. Meeting the standards set by the supervisory ministry, department or agency for the listed exporting produce would mean an added value to what are produced in the farms. The diversification of government into agricultural productions and services are openers for professionals to start earning and creating more wealth. A farmer of yam that used to produce on two acres of land initially would be motivated by the policy to cultivate more acres of land to grow the income. The mobile trainers of agro-based value chains in form of organizing seminars is a way of making income.

IMPROVE YOUR SKILL AND DIVERSIFY TO KEEP GROWING YOUR WEALTH

All professional artisans could learn additional skills to enrich their brilliance on the job. The improved intellectual capacity of the artisans is required to boost quality service and products. Unfortunately, the low patronage of many is ignorantly attached to a diabolical challenge otherwise called spiritual attack or the magical or voodoo effect of evil eyes on their jobs. Nay, this notion is absolutely wrong and archaic in the modern world of business. Such needs not to be living under a spell or believe so. He simply needs encouragement (bravery and confidence) to brace up to tackle the challenges headlong as they appear. It should be a process of solving a problem before another or taking a right step to end a scourge before another.

In some cases, a step could be the solution to solve all problems at a time. On the part of a nation suffering economic crises, right policies and full implementation could solve all the problems at a go. Sometimes, increasing the sources of earning could solve all major problems that have to do with funds. On the part of the artisans aiming at improving the sources of income, there are steps to take. They need to learn about the strategies adopted by the successful business institutions within and abroad. In this clime by observation, instead of learning from workshops and seminars or a critical studying of other business services or products to learn new things, the failing business owners used to rescind to fate. A tailor in the poor nations is poor simply because of lack of creativity to innovate strategic ideas on the building and marketing of the service to different segments of the population within and outside the shore in the modern trend. A tailor should always think outside the box. He or she could produce in Nigeria and locate the buyers abroad if he can learn to discover the tastes of those target customers there vice versa. With the use of online and internet services, the tastes of different markets could be known to the tailors for him to design what could fetch him forex.

By this, his wealth would be improved upon. Limitless are the opportunities before the artisans from different professional leanings. He could adopt 'design, sow and supplies' directly to selected clients at different institutions. Assuming a tailor could engage in home and mobile service, running tailoring school or vocational class for different segments of pupils; he could run home training for the pupils at formal schools as part of their extra curriculum activities to build entrepreneurial spirits in the pupils for a service charge or could open fashion reality shows for fashion products exhibitions to attract big clients and instant sales; he could partner with the promoters of entertainment sectors, film producers to supply the costumes for the thespians and the artistes among others. One can imagine countless ways that a tailor could be making more wealth from the line of added value jobs.

INVEST IN PROFIT ENHANCING BUSINESS

Many investors that fail in their bid to expand their business network into surest path of return on capital employed. Investors must not be in a hurry to invest if growing of the wealth of the companies is the company objective. What is the sense in a business to invest part of its earning on business that would stagnate the revenue or run at a loss? Business must not take any financial risk. Pay-back period (PBP) of the capital should be the topmost priority to grow the profits. The risks in any investment should be rightly taken on such investments that would surely bring the returns. Firms in firm should be those that would add values to the profits and not otherwise. This is the reason for the companies that are producing complementary and supplementary products. Running departmental stores in a mall owned by a parent firm is a way to enrich the profits and grow the wealth of the business.

INVEST IN SPORTS, TOURISM AND TRADITIONAL CULTURES

Nigeria is a nation whose huge population like sports especially football. There are selected books or prints that are largely accepted. Lovers of English teams used to travel to watch live Premiership matches of their darling teams. They largely patronize their insignias. These include the sports tabloids and sports-related activities. Nigerians like relaxation and could spend fortune to get this attained. There are different approaches to make wealth from the sports, tourism and cultures. First, government should license private institutions to present proposals on how to rebrand the sports sectors with the use English Football Management as a template for the use of the committees for the rebranding of the league for each of the tiers. The template should consider private ownership of sports facilities for rent or lease to the teams that may not be able to own its own at outset of clubs registrations.

Secondly, government could use the popular stars from the nation who are known in the world of sports to win international contests if they become the faces of the individual sports and therefore the government should empower the sports federations to host all the sports for the nation, region, continent and the world. If football has contests at all levels for the age groups within the nation in the football calendar, this would spread the wealth being generated from all the areas that are directly and indirectly connected with the sport. The sector shall attract private investors from all over the world as it is doing to the United Kingdom environment in particular. Flexible policies that would promote all the sports should be put in place for all the stakeholders to have the chance to generate wealth across the boards.

On the issue of promoting tourism, Nigerians love leisure and several places of attraction to relax. One cannot rightly say the percentage of the nationals that enjoy and could spend huge sum on relaxation. If the tourist places in the states of the federation are well rebranded for international community, no state would generate less than 100,000 in a year as an average number. In a year, tourism would fetch the nation huge sum of money and create more wealth from injections into the economy from foreigners within the region and the world in general.

What about the traditional cultures of ethno-religion values? They are another source of investments that would boost hospitality business across the federation. In southwest Nigeria for instance, there are several tourist promoting ethno-religion festivals that would have positive impacts on all other sectors of the economy. Some examples are Ojude Oba Day in Ijebu Ode, Durbar in the ancient city of Kano and other North East and North West of the nation, the Argungun festivals in Birni Kebbi, Eyo masquerades and Lagos Carnival in Lagos, Calabar carnival in Cross river state used to pull crowds and fun lovers from across the world. The hosts should package what could generate income to the nation for sale at places of attractions. All the festivals need repackaging by the information and culture ministry to attract crowds from within and abroad to generate forex.

ENGAGE IN DISTRIBUTION BUSINESS

Many retailers are poor simply because of their stagnancy waiting for customers that may never come. They make barely gain that would sustain their own mouths not to talk of many members and meeting several other financial responsibilities among the list of the essentials not to talk of other social needs. They are getting poorer simply because limited customers would patronize their stand beyond their expectation. They simply lack the strategies to move their product around to places where the target customers are got. Many hawkers on the streets may make huge sum as gain but would hardly fund health crises.

Let me use a simple illustration. The hawkers along the highways cover several hundreds of kilometres running after vehicles every day under different weather conditions. They would never mind the body cuts they have in the cause of making 'huge sales'. Assume such makes 5,000 in a day. If he falls sick suddenly, diagnoses and tests may cost more than 20,000 naira not to talk of the medical fees to the medical staff for the hospital. Distribution is far better a strategy to hawk with decency and record heavy sales towards making huge profits. The gains can be grown as more targets are met in customers. I used to envy the bulk distributors of books and related items in Europe. The distributors of books to libraries and bookstores would continue to generate more profits as the number of customer soars and the stores keeping adding to the types of stock of books they demanded through the company. If a distributor distributes 10,000 of a title in a month and the number of titles selected and preferred by the customers are ten. If the average demand of the books per quarter is 100,000 of all the books; such has the ability to increase the units by double if he is able to cover or win more buyers in bookstores and libraries. Improve your earning via distributing essentials like foods and ingredients to hotels, eateries, restaurants at different places like schools, hospitals, parks, markets, malls etc. Distribute newspapers, magazines, professional journals of different brands and features to selected places. This is far better than appealing for patronage from the unknown customers as shopless and loitering (itinerant) hawker.

CREATE BOOK READING ENVIRONMENT

Nigeria is a nation whose population read materials a lot but not much of the printed books. Students, in most cases, do read books to excel in their examinations. In the latter, it that has low reading culture compare to the advanced nations whose population read books across different themes widely. In books are secrets of the world. In books are found the secrets of life and good living. In books are inspiration to excel in all life challenges. People who read used to have choices of books to read. Many read motivational books only. The religionist used to patronize religion-based books and materials. The youths who are still learning about sex education used to read sex education and the related in books. Managers' source for managerial enhanced books as the lawyers read tomes of law books from different courts and the interpretations of the learned professionals. One simple fact is that whether people like it or not, we read books and would continue to read books. Medical doctors like the judge and the men of the silk would continue to consult their books like the consultancies of different professions.

All the researchers and economic think tanks must read to be up and doing on the nature of their jobs towards quality delivery. The lecturers and the facilitators are some of the stakeholders who could force people to develop reading habits, love and interestingly read books that some have become bookworms or funnily called 'encyclopedia'. With this huge populace, the nation could generate a lot of money even forex from promoting the reading culture and the rebranding the libraries. If the library is seen as social and profit-making business, the book industry would be adequately patronized. Through the sector, several businesses shall be easily created with billions of income in hard currency on annual basis. One can imagine the amount of royalties for the authors who are constantly churning out interesting books on different aspects of life and living! Wealth would be created, new jobs shall be equally be at the beck and calls of the youths that are roaming the streets in search of jobs. government could enhance reading culture by creating libraries and relax places especially meant for reading across the nooks and corners of the nation especially in schools at all levels of education.

GETTING POOR YOUR OWN WAY

The reverse of the above sub-theme is the content that could turn a professional poor in the midst of opportunities. Over-dependent on others when people, institutions and government failure to think on how to be self-reliance cripple them the more and render them poor. In a family where the father is the sole breadwinner, they would live in abject poverty. The poor decisions of individual and institutions even government could render them poor for life. We can say that Africans are to blame their post-independence leaders and poor values including intolerance for their economic and political backwardness and not the colonial masters and the advanced nations. They choose to be poor and poorer when other nations at the opposite bloc choose to be rich and richer. These are caused by the thirst for power for personal enrichment via looting and all forms of corruption at the expense of the nations and the nationals. Poor decisions and policies of governments continue to render the nations poor and poorer by the day. It also applies to private business institutions that are closing every day for low or no patronage.

In fact, the opportunity of being at the helms is a great opportunity in a lifetime. Being owner of a business institution is a lifetime opportunity. Being an expert in a field is an opportunity to grow wealth. Being recognized with a skill is a path to glory, fame and riches. Being physically and mentally strong is an added value to what one has obtained, inherited and bestowed with in endowments. It is very ludicrous seeing people who have all the limbs and mentally sound begging for money or food in a street when he has opportunity to seek for menial job for sustaining at the moment. The physically challenged could be trained to be self-reliant and earning legally from the skills they had acquired or naturally endowed with. They could be given similar opportunities as those given to the able-body people. In the right clime, there are sports for the disable just as they used to organize for the able-body people of all gender. It is a mistake on the part of a talented or skilled physically challenged to resort into alms begging from the charity givers outside the streets. It is nation that is bereft of think tanks that fails to recognize the inputs and contributions of the disable to the wealth of the nation. In the midst are good examples from the disable world. Nigeria has talented musician **Dan Maraya of Jos** (of blessed memory) like the France **Steve Wonders** of this world. Through the singer recognized for his talent, his family is taken care of from the legitimate source courtesy the accepted songs from the singer. How can a sane man sell all his inherited property to invest in a journey abroad seeking green pasture? A travelling agent friend once told me that it costs as much as over one million naira to travel abroad when such amount is not even needed to establish businesses that would earn him money in the nation. All the vacuums created by the inability or inefficiency (deficiencies) of government are open for investors to make huge sums of income legally.

Imagine a company that relocates or situates its business into a volatile area. What would happen to the business in times of confrontations? The choice of wrong product or service is a wrong step for a business at outset. A noble guide from the lip of the noblest is to avoid a place that is diseased or has an epidemic and never leave a place where there is epidemic if you are there at the time'. There is wisdom in this saying. Have understanding of the business environment before you make investment decisions. A capitalist that is financially prudent would not invest blindly but cautiously and wisely with time after considering several dynamics. All verifiable data showing concise information about the location or the business environment must be studied before investment is done as part of the pre-investment task. Wrong decisions could lower the income if the liquidation is not set in.

On the part of human beings, man fails to understand self before rescinding to unknown fate. Do you ever see whom you are by physical feature before a standing mirror? Do you ever critically assess your natural endowments? Do you ever identify such jobs you can start with zero or mere little capital? Do you ever care to understand what the society needs for you to provide as a money earning job? Secondly, most who are poor lack of self-contentment and this could lead to perpetual poverty instead of garner necessary guides to be rich and grow the riches. Inability to sieve the physical and spiritual attacks could be the reason for being poor for individual. How can a being be comparing self with mates whose sources of income are unknown or tainted with question mark? After all, fingers are never equal. No man is 'own all' but man is natural 'have little' and 'seek others'. What a man has in abundance, another lacks vice versa. I laughed when my people cast the economic decline of the nation to the festivals of arts and culture in 1977 by Obasanjo military administration. The incorruptible scriptures guide us to look within ourselves before attributing blames. Many ills befalling us are self-inflict but we like to cast the blame on one another. Endless are the instances to establish this stand from the day to day events in this clime. We have seen newly married low earning couple who prefer to live in the midst of the rich even though their income is less than average. Their tastes are too high for what they earn. A big earning man is married to one wife but 'servicing' several concubines outside he got at beer drinking joint and clubs. And his only source of money is the same business. Would his earning be increasing or getting depleting by the day? Have you heard of people and institutions even government that live above their incomes? Yes, there are. They pretend to be what they are not. They are poor yet pretending to be big. They live a life of deception. Many hire cars and live in exotic places to show class they never belong. What a chameleon in the skin of men!

A family has a problem with finance to meet the family needs. The family found it difficult to pay rent of 48,000 naira for a two room apartment rented. They made effort to relocate to a room in order to reduce the annual rent to 12,000 naira. After few years, they found it difficult again to pay for the 12,000 naira rent. Then, some people advised them to relocate to their uncompleted house at about ten kilometres away to the town. Some amount was raised by the extended family and they agreed to relocate. This movement had rendered them poorer than before as the family spent 400 on transportation each day. This amounted to 12,000 in a month an amount that would have offset a year rent in the city where they would have access to all social amenities. It is established from outset that everyone has the potential to improve on their earnings from application of the senses and some efforts. Many people in business are in debts for running poor business decisions as a result of lack of vision or determined objective to serve as focus. If a professional set a target of making certain sum as profits per month, his mission is to double the efforts and inputs, at least, such should be able to achieve additional profits from the initial ones. If a business targets one million from the previous 500,000 earning at the end of an accounting period, and more efforts and better strategies are put in place, such could make not less than 700,000 and the wealth shall continue to grow by each accounting period as efforts and inputs are constantly introduced. In fact, their debts keep soaring by the day. Some go to the extent of committing suicide. Many flee from their creditors after failure to pay or service their debts. One would wonder the reason for the defaulting debtors despite huge sales being recorded by their sales outlets.

Research showed different causes. A woman is into catering and event planning business. She has training institute where apprenctices are being trained to become caterers and planners to. She used to collect fees for the training. Unknowingly or out of ignorance, she has to expand her business with some loans from the micro finance houses. She was lured into borrowing huge sum of money beyond her business need at the time. Instead of working on how to expand and diversify into other value added jobs, she received the capital with the stringent condition and use huge part on the building personal building at a new site. Do you see the three business mistakes she had committed? What are these business mistakes? One, she failed to learn to understand the conditions attached to the loan. Two, she lacked the actual area of business interest to invest one for her ill-preparation. Three, she used a capital that was meant to generate profits on a project that would be a liability till the end of the project. Building a house from the capital meant for business is a business mistake. A business invested upon fetch the investor profits unlike a house at outset. Instead of building a house, a shopping mall that would host her catering service and others who rent or lease should have been a better business strategy for her. Alas, she squandered the money into wrong venture. By this, she runs into debt for many years now!

Observation of the market situations from the retailing business and salary earners shows the ignorance of the traders and the salaried workers on how to beef up their sources of incomes at different periods. Many do not know that as the children are growing, the financial demands to support the families would automatically increase. These are families whose sources of income have been a stable ones for years even before marriage. Those who are selling at retail do not deem it fit to increase the volumes of sales by increasing the number of brands or rise to become wholesaler or joining both retailing and wholesaling to earn more money to maintain the new status. Most salary earners especially in private companies suffer more for non-review of the remuneration by their employers. The public servant used to have periodical upward review of the salaries. The new minimum wage act and the social welfare package for the workers could be said to be a way of increasing earning but the otherwise is the case. The rising inflation always render the upward review irrelevant. As the expenses on the family increases as inflation rises with the same income, they drop in the standard of living.

In the early 2000, three telecoms mobile operators were issued licenses by the nation's communication commission. Six others joined the business later. Within the first three years, one of them had changed ownership and brand names thrice. By the year 2016, only four were in the market. And they are claiming to be running at low pace as a result of dwindling patronage hence profits. Before the starting of the second half of the year, one of the great four closed its shop but opened another owner to take over the baton. In simple words, the end of a business is the source of another brand of business.

Without doubt, people easily rescind to fate. Firms that are mono-product or service would face liquidation when competitors arrive into the market. A nation that is mono-lithic could face economy decline in the wake of low patronage of the product. This is an experience of Nigeria in the recent. Students do not aim at starting a business idea. Most of them prefer white collar jobs. The artisans used to abandon the trade for work-and-eat jobs like commercial riders on the roads. Many have become construction workers. By engaging in these menial jobs at the expense of their artisanal jobs, the income gets lower and standard of living constantly drops.

CHAPTER FOUR

GAINS TO THE NATIONAL ECONOMY

All should have interest in the creation of more wealth through grabbing opportunities to promote diversifications into new products and services. The citizens and the private business institutions including the nation have the chance to enhance their wealth. Nations could grow the income from low into high income for better per capita income with the effective use of the opportunities at their beck and call. The giant stride of the Singaporean President that transformed the nation from the third world into first world is always a reference point for nations. Eliminate corruption namely financial, moral and spiritual corruption from the garbs of individuals at all positions of authorities, the nation in distress would start to earn more and increase the volumes of trades and hence earnings in incomes or revenues. A good policy of government could catalyze the wealth creation of all the stakeholders in the poor nation. Let us cite some samples. A poor nation could empower all tertiary and allied schools, with funds and equipment, to have their own demonstration farms where staple and cash crops are produced in large plantation. By this, the nation would be food sufficient. With the excess, the agro-based businesses would grow and the number of industries employing huge numbers of employees shall grow within a short space of time. Reform financial institutions that forbid illicit transfers of funds under money laundering act could end the withdrawals from the economies. If a nation embraces the information and communication technology by opening national e-market place where all products and services including the links to the owners are placed, there would be mass patronage and more earnings for the makers and service patrons across the nation even if there is less from outside the shores. A nation like Nigeria that has huge consumption rate with a population of almost 180 million is big enough as a market to turn the producers and the service providers into millionaires if the patronage of local products is put at even 50%. Promotion of the patronage of the locally-manufactured and produced raw materials by the government and institutions who truly live by examples would boost the production and money earning of the factories. The promotion from the media organs of the government and the continue sensitization as in the use of national platform of e-market place at a cheap fee of subscription would be a motivation for all round production by all and sundry.

On the other angle, the failure in the administration to run a balanced budget on the basis of what is available is always a path to open eyes of individuals into how to grow their wealth. In the book "**Wastes to Wealth jobs**" by the same author, we exposed how nations, despite their challenges that are sources of wealth generation for the visionary leaders, could brace up and create rooms for the citizens and institutions into wealth creation. A dirty environment in a nation has prompted private owned wastes managers to be earning from evacuation and recycling of solid wastes. Numerous are the gains of the topic to the nation. When education system is recording failures from the mass failure of pupils in examinations, this has created rooms for private tutors and new schools after schools to increase their incomes. The deficit budget of a government is an avenue for private institutions to increase their wealth from concessionaire arrangement to build social infrastructures. If the proposals to build and manage before transfer of highways to the government is signed by the construction companies and toll gates are located to collect tolls, the income of the companies have been enriched. An investor local and foreign that has the relevant information about the business environment shall be able to increase the wealth in the nation. Those who are endowed with the brains and hearts are the pacesetters. They create new jobs from the rubbles and particularly from the added value chains of their jobs. We can say that the decision to get wealthy by one's way is like creating new jobs from the existing jobs. By their efforts, new employments are created. Government could generate wealth from the transformation of the physically challenged into the acquirement of artisanal skills. A right environment that would catalyze the innate resources of these people shall add to the wealth. Spending on them without making any gain from their inputs shall be otherwise. Nations can also convert the sentenced inmates to life imprisonment inmates into different artisanal jobs and agricultural-based jobs in order to enhance the wealth of the nation. Otherwise, the nation would continue to spend heavily on the liabilities. Leaders of huge vision would prefer turning the inmates into wealth creators and not a parasite to the nation's treasury.

CHAPTER FIVE

BOOSTING THE SECTORS IN THE TIME OF RECESSION

As taught in one of the chapters earlier, all opportunities created by prevalent challenges especially when the nation is suffering from economic downturn open the windows of wealth creating opportunities.

A fact is that challenges shall be continually created for the think tanks to churn out jobs and create wealth. During recession period, opportunities to generate wealth become more glaring. My researches about the environment revealed how millions can be created at a swap with the reviews of the policies for each of the sectors. The tertiary schools could be financially independent with the conversion of the intellectual property in the institution into wealth creation. The arts and theatre department can develop scripts to produce block buster films that would attract huge revenues. The books written by the endowed writers from all departments could be published in the school's website and special commercial site to earn regular income. The research papers and theses are materials for wealth generation. What about the faculty of agriculture towards developing agricultural economy? Each of the departments in the faculty could transform all the students and the lecturers into producers of farm produce of cash and food crops, fish, bees, domesticated rats and other domesticated animals and birds. In our work **'Wastes to wealth'**, it is made clear that all things can be converted as wealth and equally generate millions of employments. If the tertiary and allied schools could engage in practical demonstration of their works with the use of acquired land by government for the process and industrial layouts for small processing companies, wealth shall be created at all the sectors. The built of film villages at different location for the schools and the independent makers shall boost entertainment sector. Each of the institutions and the professional associations could be empowered by amendments of acts to create more wealth. A nation that fails to engage and task all institutions through enabling policies would remain poor.

We can use the same for institutions across the boards. It takes the right thinking people at the helms of the institutions to review the companies' stakes in the markets as far as the growth of the business are concerned.

CHAPTER SIX
EMPLOYMENT GENERATION AND IMPROVING STANDARD OF LIVING

The greatest gain of the ability to generate wealth through the diversifications by individuals, institutions and governments at all tiers is the variants of new jobs that shall be created for the people. The developed nations that are blessed with visionary leaders and strong institutions not to talk of independent investors that enjoy enabling policies and right business environment would always create more wealth. The underdeveloped nations could learn from the advanced economies to start building wealth and grow it with stable enhancing policies. Individuals can discover and invest of talents and natural skills of the members of the family to turn them into additional sources of income for the family. If a man identifies a skill in a child in the family, he should invest to horn the skill in order to make additional income for self and the family. One can imagine what football and other sports talents across the advanced nations are making for their families today. The wise investments of the earnings from the talents shall continually add to the jobs in the nations. Each investor of business institutions that is continually develops new products and services by these strategic investments. Through the diversification as a measure to boost the wealth of the companies, new jobs are created for staff and unskilled jobs. The public institutions under the government would continue to have positive impact in the employment markets by the continual provision of new jobs directly and indirectly. This is doable in a way to continual increasing their wealth of riches and other resources.

The football as a sport in the European nation has created several millions of jobs for direct and indirect workers.

ABOUT THE BOOK

This book, is a semblance of the bestselling title **'Getting rich your own way'** written by **Brian Tracy**. The presentation serves as a source of inspiration teaching **'Getting wealthy your own way'** legitimately. This is a title specially chosen and whose contents teach how to individuals, institutions and nations could amass wealth at their own pace no matter the challenges.

The major difference in the contents of the two books remains that the former has America and Europe setting while the latter uses the developing and underdeveloped environment as case studies. The contents of the book depict, with illustrations, on how the people regardless of gender, race, age, affiliation, academic qualifications, social status; the institutions and the nations in such places could amass wealth in riches, skills and other resources vice versa.

The book shows how all the citizens could add their own quotas to the wealth of the nation. It maintains that failure for individuals, institutions and governments at all tiers would result into liabilities and a drain in the nation's treasury.

The book is an asset to all students learning to start new business ideas; the entrepreneurs, the business institutions and the visionary leaders at government levels through the ministries, departments and agencies as an inevitable guide to boost the wealth of the beneficiaries.

ABOUT THE AUTHOR

He is a motivational speaker, socio-economic think tank, researcher, prolific writer and author of series of books. His range of books include the entrepreneurial books like **'Jobs with zero capital'** in two volumes, **'Creating new jobs from the existing jobs**; philosophical and inspirational books like 'Words are absolutely powerful' and 'Ask'. He wrote books on economy and these include 'Understanding business environment, right or wrong; 'A concise perspective of understanding Nigeria business environment, right or wrong; 'Piracy, the causes, the trends, the spiral adverse effects and practicable solutions' among others. He is married with kids and a product of citadel of technological innovations, The Polytechnic Ibadan.

RECOMMENDED BOOKS

Amusa Abdulateef (2017) Path from the fourth world to the first world nation Addin Resources Ventures Ibadan Nigeria www.amusa-abdulteef.com

Ditto (2017) Over 200 reasons why abundantly rich nations are poor Addin Resources Ventures Ibadan, Nigeria www.amusa-abdulateef.com

www.ingramcontent.com/pod-product-compliance
Lightning Source LLC
Chambersburg PA
CBHW031546210526
45464CB00003B/1173